D1133177

PAUL CUFFE
AND THE
AFRICAN
PROMISED LAND

PAUL CUFFE
AND THE
AFRICAN
PROMISED LAND

by Mary Gage Atkin

THOMAS NELSON INC., PUBLISHERS

Nashville
New York

First edition

Library of Congress Cataloging in Publication Data

Atkin, Mary Gage.
  Paul Cuffe and the African promised land.

  Includes index.
  SUMMARY: A biography of the Afro-American sea captain who
sought to attract freed blacks from America to the colony of Sierra
Leone.
    1. Cuffe, Paul, 1759-1817—Juvenile literature. 2. Afro-Amer-
icans—Biography—Juvenile literature. 3. Sierra Leone—History—
Juvenile literature. [1. Cuffe, Paul, 1759-1817. 2. Afro-Americans
—Biography. 3. Sierra Leone—History] I. Title.
E185.97.C96A84   973.4′092′4 [B] [92]   76-26607
ISBN 0-8407-6521-5

my first book
for
my firstborn,
Amory

CONTENTS

PAUL CUFFE

AND THE

AFRICAN
PROMISED LAND

PROLOGUE –
Cuffe Slocum

Now he was a man. A free man. He belonged to himself. As a boy in Ghana he had belonged to a tribe. But before he could become a man in Ghana, he had been taken to Massachusetts to belong to a white man. He had been Captain Ebenezer Slocum's slave for fifteen years. He had stayed a boy for those fifteen years. He had done a man's work all that time, but he wasn't a man. Captain Slocum had bought a ten-year-old boy. And the captain had kept him a "boy," who just worked, ate, and slept. He wasn't a man. He was a stabled animal taken out to work from dawn to dusk and then shut up again until the next working dawn.

He labored, and Captain Slocum enjoyed the fruits of that labor. And he worked hard, because if he didn't, Captain Slocum could sell him into a worse life. He could sell him to a plantation on the Gulf of Mexico, where slaves were quickly worked to death. He was a good worker for the captain, but still he was sold. Luckily he wasn't sold down the river. He was sold to John Slocum. It was like a reward. John Slocum was a good master.

He paid £150 for the twenty-five-year-old slave "Cuffe" and then let his new slave work off his purchase price. With freedom for his goal, Cuffe doubled his work load. He completed his master's daily assigned tasks, then took whatever odd jobs he could find. In less than three years his master went to the squire to have a paper drawn up granting Cuffe Slocum his freedom.

The next morning the squire brought the document to John Slocum. He asked Cuffe if he wanted to be a free man. Then he took the paper out of his pocket and read it to Cuffe. Mr. and Mrs. Slocum signed their names, and the squire declared Cuffe a free man. He told him to live a steady life and take good care of the money he was going to earn and save it so he could get a home sometime. The squire and John Slocum both then offered Cuffe a job with wages.

Cuffe Slocum thanked them. His tears fell on his precious freedom paper, and he tucked it in his shirt. He packed his two everyday suits of clothes and left immediately to become his own man and start a new life.

He never once looked back. The rain fell and mixed with his tears. He noticed neither. He was reborn—a free man! But he didn't want to be free and alone. He wanted to be a free family man. A few months later he became engaged to Ruth Moses, a Gay Head Indian girl. And on July 7, 1746, less than two years after he became free, Cuffe Slocum was married.

1

Paul

Cuffe went to live with his wife's tribe. The Gay Head Indians were descended from the once powerful Wampanoag tribe, who had helped the Pilgrims survive their first winter in Plymouth. They taught the white man how to grow corn, sweet potatoes, pumpkins, and cranberries, and how to hunt the wild turkey. In return, the Pilgrims pushed the Wampanoags back from Plymouth Bay to their western boundary along Narragansett Bay. Beyond the bay was the land of their neighbors, the Narragansett Indians. The Wampanoags could retreat no farther.

The Pilgrims saw the Wampanoags' land as an area "vast and unpeopled . . . fruitful and fitt for habitation, being devoyd of all civil inhabitants, where there are only savage and brutish men, which range up and down, little otherwise than the wild beasts." The Pilgrims saw the Indians as savages, as something less than human. Therefore, they could be killed just like the other wild animals in America.

The Indians saw the Pilgrims as intruders and violators of "this mother of ours," the land. No one could own the land, and "we therefore yield to our neighbors, even our animal neighbors, the same right as ourselves to inhabit this land." The Wampanoags believed the land to be abundant enough to support everyone, and their sachems pledged peace so both races could dwell together.

But the Pilgrims didn't want to dwell with the Wampanoags. They pushed the Indians farther and farther west, and in 1676, in the so-called King Philip's War, they set out to destroy their power for good. Before the fighting was over twelve Indian villages had been wiped out and one out of every sixteen men of military age killed.

The remnants of the Wampanoags settled off the coast of their homeland on the tiny Elizabeth Islands in Buzzard's Bay. Cuffe Slocum moved with his new wife to Cuttyhunk, one of the largest and most populous of the Elizabeths. Cuttyhunk's 516 acres were blessed with fertile soil and dense woods. Here, among the proud independent Wampanoags, Cuffe Slocum farmed, fished, and raised ten children, four boys and six girls.

The fourth boy, Paul, was born on a cold January 17 in the year 1759. He inherited his father's diligence and his mother's proud independent spirit. His father taught him to work hard. His mother's people taught him how to live from the land and the sea. They taught him the Indian way through patient example instead of the Puritan way through guilt and fear. The Puritans believed that sparing the rod meant spoiling the child. The Indians believed in close ties between parents and children. So Paul grew up fearless and self-sufficient.

But Cuffe Slocum wanted more than just freedom for his children. He knew the value the white man placed on property. The Indians he lived among revered the land, but they had lost it. New England was now the white man's country. And only property owners could succeed in the white man's world.

Cuffe Slocum had bought physical freedom for his children. Now he wanted to buy financial freedom for them as well. To do that, he would have to leave the

Indians and earn money in the white man's world. He moved his family to Martha's Vineyard, settling them near the little town of Chilmark. He worked hard. And it was not long before he had the substantial sum of 650 Spanish milled dollars to buy a 120-acre farm in Westport, Massachusetts.

In the bleak, closing days of 1766, Cuffe Slocum sailed his family across the rough wintry stretch of ocean separating Martha's Vineyard from the mainland. But even colder than their Atlantic crossing was the welcome they received upon their arrival at Westport. The village was an established, fairly prosperous farming and fishing community. Very few blacks lived there. And those few were mostly bondmen, household servants.

The whites of Westport were not very familiar with free blacks and tended to regard all blacks as inferior. Cuffe Slocum worked so hard to overcome the discrimination in Westport that within six years of his move there, he was dead. The thirteen-year-old Paul and his older brother John inherited the family farm and the responsibility of providing for a widowed mother and three younger sisters. Paul was as concerned as his father had been for the family's well-being. He worked as hard as his father had on the farm. But unlike his father, Paul stood up to the discrimination in Westport and protested it by changing the family's name. He dropped the white slave owner's name of Slocum and replaced it with his father's name, Cuffe. So now the family of Cuffe Slocum was known simply as the Cuffes.

2

Whaling

Paul Cuffe wanted more than his father's hard-won freedom. He wanted equality, and equality was not possible on land. He looked to the sea. Surely at sea things weren't black or white—just blue. He would be a seaman. His father was born on the Gulf of Guinea, where New England whalemen had been following the whales since 1763 and had discovered that the best harpooners, steersmen, and all-round whalemen were the Africans from the Bissagos Islands in the Guinea Basin.

His mother's people, the Gay Head Indians, had always been skilled fishermen. They taught the sea-fearing, land-loving colonists how to hunt the black right whales that migrated south in the fall off Gay Head on the western end of Martha's Vineyard. When the Indian lookouts along the coast sighted the "bedagi," they made a great noise and launched their canoes to try to trap a whale in a canoe-formed semicircle against the shore.

Then an Indian arose in the prow of each canoe. He raised a long, heavy shaft with an eighteen-inch harpoon at its fore end. The harpoon was made either of polished bone or fire-hardened wood set with very sharp, slender, recurved stone teeth. Long lines of twisted well-greased fiber hung from the harpoon head. The lines lay coiled in the bottom of the canoe attached to four-foot lengths of light logs or inflated bladders made of deer or dog skin tightly sewn and sealed with rosin.

As the whale surfaced in response to the shouting, banging, drumming, and screaming, the nearest Indians hurled their harpoons directly down into its shining black back. The other canoes shot forward to sink their harpoons until the blood-flooded sea was covered with bobbing bladders. The great whale moaned and thrashed about in its death agony, capsizing canoes and scattering Indians in great confusion. Finally its huge bulk stilled and floated like a gigantic shadow just beneath the surface, buoyed up by the inflated bladders attached to its body.

After the kill, a silence fell over the tribe. Then the men hauled the whale onto the beach while the women made a roaring fire. The meat was eaten and the bones cleaned for future building purposes. The blubber and other uneaten portions were melted down for lighting, cooking, and medicinal oil. The English navigator Captain Waymouth wrote in 1605:

> When the Indians have killed the whale and dragged him to shore, they call all their chief lords together and sing a song of joy; and those chief lords, whom they call sagamores, divide the spoil and give to every man a share, which pieces are distributed, they hang up about their houses for provisions; and when they boil them they blow off the fat and put their pease, maize and other pulse which they eat.

The early colonists, who scorned the Indians as ignorant savages, were quick to copy their whaling skills. They already knew the value of whale oil. Before the discovery of petroleum, lamps had to burn animal oil, and all oil was scarce and costly. The charter given to the

Pilgrims aboard the Mayflower granted them "all royal fishes, whales, balan, sturgeons and other fishes."

The Pilgrims decided to stay on Cape Cod Bay because "every day we saw whales plying hard by us; of which in that place, if we had instruments and means to take them we might make a very rich return. Our master and his mates professed we might make three or four thousand pounds worth of oil."

Years later when one of the King's commissioners was sent to investigate economic conditions in the colonies, he wrote home that "New Plymouth Colony have great profit by whale killing. I believe it will be one of our best returnes." But Massachusetts was too greedy. By law one third of every whale went to the town and one third to the church. As for the Indian, the law stated that: "whosoever hires an Indian to go a-whaling shall not give him above one trucking cloath coat for each whale he and his company shall kill, or half the blubber without the whalebone."

In Nantucket things were different. To the Indians it was "Nanticut"—meaning "the faraway land." To the Quaker settlers of 1658, it was a haven from the religious intolerance of Massachusetts. The Quakers bought land from the Indians and divided it equally among themselves. They planted crops, built log cabins with thatched roofs, and watched the Indians hunt whales. Deciding that canoes capsized too easily, they invited the expert boatman, Ichabod Paddock of Cape Cod, to help them improve on the Indians' whaling techniques.

Ichabod devised long clinker-built rowboats with several sets of oars that rode the waves without tipping. Then he set up a series of tall coastal watchtowers manned by the islanders on a voluntary basis. As soon as whales were spotted, the Quakers and Indians launched the rowboats together and killed the whales the Indian way, except that the harpoons were made of iron instead of stone.

Together they towed the hundred-ton whales to shore through Nantucket's terrific coastal tide, rips, currents, and pounding surf. A "crab" or shore winch hauled the whale's body ashore so the blubber could be stripped from all sides and boiled or "tryed out" in large iron pots. The baleen was cleaned, trimmed, and softened in hot water, then sold for ladies' corset stays. The meat, which the white man didn't eat, the bones, and the rest of the carcass was given to the Indians. They rendered the remains and got a lot of oil for their own use.

In Nantucket the whaling industry, like the land, was communally owned and worked on a cooperative basis, with each man receiving a portion commensurate with the work he had done. Later, when the right whales disappeared from the coast, the men of Nantucket built sloops and then schooners to hunt the whale up north to the Grand Banks and south to the Gulf and Caribbean. But they extended the same cooperative system, known as the "lay system," for use on board the sailing ships, with everyone sharing in the proceeds of the voyage.

Many mainlanders came to the island where all men were equal and worked equally hard for their own profit. Blacks came also, because there was no slavery in Nantucket. They clustered in the south part of Nantucket, built their own church and school, and became excellent whalemen and such valuable members of the crew that many had become officers by the early nineteenth century.

In 1761 Joseph Russell laid out a plan for a village on his Massachusetts land. Four years later Joseph Rotch, a whaling merchant from Nantucket, joined Russell to make a whaling port of his village of New Bedford. Within ten years eighty whaling ships with Nantucket men and ways were sailing up the Acushnet River to their new home port on the mainland.

There weren't enough men from the island of Nantucket to man all the ships, so new hands were always needed. Anyone able and willing to learn was accepted, for everyone, black, red, or white, was equal on a Nantucket ship. Paul Cuffe was able, and Paul Cuffe wanted to learn. He had taught himself to read and write on the farm. Now, at sixteen, he wanted to be a "marineer."

Sustained by his mother's Indian pride and his father's determination to succeed, Paul walked eight miles from the farm village of Westport to the whaling port of New Bedford. It was a far shorter journey than his father had traveled for a new life. And New Bedford was new. Instead of shops and carts filled with farm produce and the smell of manure, there was the smell of tar, hemp, and fish. There were cooperages, which made the barrels, sail lofts, which cut and sewed the sails, a smithy to forge the harpoons, and ship chandlers' stores with all the gear, goods, and food needed for an ocean voyage.

Near the wooden wharves were heavy-timbered warehouses full of hundreds of casks of oil. More barrels covered the wharves. As Paul threaded his way among them, his eye was caught by a beautiful bark. Her three masts pointed proudly above the single masts of the smaller sloops and schooners that crowded nearly hull to hull around her. She lay moored in the middle of the river like a queen with her subjects around her. That was the ship Paul wanted to sail on. So he did.

The bark was bound for the Gulf of Mexico to hunt the valuable sperm whale, the mighty warrior of the seas. The sperm whale is a sixty-foot fighter with huge teeth. It fights to feed on the giant squid and octopus, near the bottom of warm and temperate seas. It fights to collect and keep a harem. It fights those who hunt it. It can and does swallow whalers and smash their boats head on or with great blows of its powerful tail.

It is very agile and stands on its head with its tail in

the air before diving over three thousand feet straight down. It is the most difficult whale to kill but also the most valuable. Its enormous square head is filled with high-grade oil and spermaceti, a white wax from which the finest candles were made. Spermaceti candles lighted all the great cities of the Western world, for they gave a bright light that lasted all night. Its blubber gave more oil of a finer grade and its intestines contained ambergris, once worth $400 per ounce for its use in the perfume trade.

Only Nantucket-born or Nantucket-trained men hunted the great sperm whale. Their wooden ships, with their blunt bows and square transoms, may have looked small and tublike, but they served their purpose well. The far-voyaging barks, with their long, steeply cocked bow-spirits, had their fore- and mainmasts square-rigged and their mizzenmast fore-and-aft rigged to follow the migrating whales.

When Paul was rowed out to board the bark, he noticed that the ship was as organized and shipshape within as without. Forward, at the bow, was the barrel windlass for unloading the casks of whale oil. Next was the tryworks, a brick fireplace with a iron pot for rendering the blubber into oil. Abaft this was the cook's caboose or "office of the doctor," as the hands called the cook. And dominating all was the raised quarterdeck, where the captain and his mates ruled their floating kingdom.

The ship carried seventeen men quartered between decks. The captain and two mates had their cabins aft. Amidships, in steerage where the stores were stowed, were the quarters for the cooper-carpenter, who repaired the ship, and the three boat steerers or harpooners who, being specialists, were treated like unofficial under officers. Paul was directed to the fo'c'sle (forecastle) in the bows, where in a twelve-foot-square space the bunks and sea chests of ten crewmen were stowed. Here he would eat, sleep, and swap yarns until voyage's end.

Belowdecks was the hold, where the whale oil was stored in barrels made on board by the cooper from the bundles of barrel staves and rings carried in steerage. Stores and provisions were kept between decks. These had already been loaded on board, and the mate responsible for stowage was seeing that everything was arranged in precise order, according to the purpose it was to serve and the time at which it would be needed. There was the whaling equipment, the harpoons, spears, knives, and all the tools and materials required for the repair or replacement of anything broken or lost, such as sails, nails, lines, rigging, etc.

Since the ship might be at sea for months, there were also barrels of water and food—flour, molasses, rice, beans, salt beef, salt pork, and bread. And there was the medicine chest containing ointments, plasters, bicarbonate of soda, Epsom salts, and an opiate, laudanum, to kill pain. The captain was the doctor. He bled for fevers, pulled teeth, and when necessary amputated limbs. Whaling captains became quite skillful at amputation, because they had so many smashed arms and legs to practice on.

When everything had been carefully stowed, the ship inspected, and the decks cleared, the captain ordered, "Anchor apeak," and Paul and the other hands pulled and pushed at the bars of the capstan until the anchor was weighed. Topmen loosed sails, and they unfolded like flowers. The ship shook out more sail, setting her lower courses. The port of New Bedford dwindled away. The horizon opened out before the ship's bow. With all sail set, the pilot leaped nimbly into the boat that would take him back to his cutter. They were under weigh!

The first few days were spent training the seasick new hands in handling the vessel. The captain put them in the charge of his experienced Nantucket seamen and resigned himself to a clumsily handled ship for the first few days of the voyage. Paul wasn't seasick, and he learned

23

quickly all the various lines, sheets, and halyards, and which to pull on which command. He scrambled up the ratlines and sidled out along the footropes of the yards right to the end, without freezing in fright at the height. Soon he was able to keep one hand free as he climbed aloft, the rule being: "one hand for the ship, one for yourself."

But Paul wanted to learn more. He wanted to know about navigation, the prevailing winds, and the ocean currents. Nantucket whalemen were the only navigators to chart the currents. They followed the ocean currents because the whales followed them, and they followed the whales. Sperm whales liked warm currents, so the bark was following alongside the Gulf Stream straight south from New Bedford to the West Indies.

It was an uneventful voyage. There wasn't much to do but look for whales and clean the ship. They used ashes to scour the deck, because soap was available only for personal washing and fresh water was strictly rationed at sea. When not on duty Paul lay in his bunk in the forecastle and listened to the older hands tell sperm-whale tales:

"We struck a large sperm and got in three irons"—glancing at Paul—"harpoons, and one tow-iron. As soon as the tow-iron went into the whale, she gave a flank and went down, and coming up again she bolted her head out of the water almost as far as her fins. And then pitched the whole weight of her head on the boat—stove in the boat and killed the midshipman, an Indian named Sam Lamson, outright."

"Aye, but did ye hear of the great bull sperm that sank a ship. He was eighty-five feet long and came down upon the ship with full speed striking with his head just forward of the fore chains. The ship brought up violently as if she had struck a rock and started leaking badly. The whale smote his jaws together, as if distracted with rage and fury, then struck the ship directly under the cat-head and completely stove in her bows. In the space of a few minutes, the whaleship was rendered a complete wreck."

"They snap up men too—not just Jonah, Captain Gardner had a bull sperm attack his boat. The whale took it in his mouth and shook it to pieces. The captain was thrown into the air, and he fell directly into the snapping jaw of the monster. His men pulled him out. Blood poured from his mouth and his body. He had lost his left hand at the wrist and his skull was stove in. They believed him a dead man, but he recovered and is whaling still."

With no whales to catch, captains had time for visiting. The master of any passing whaleship was invariably a friend from Nantucket, who would invite their captain aboard for a "gam." Their captain would embark, in the best of his three boats, standing majestically erect between the helmsman and the stroke oar. He would receive a kingly welcome and an excellent luncheon, with much news and many experiences exchanged.

But when the whaling ground in the Gulf was reached, the ship became all business again. High aloft in the crosstrees the lookout was all eyes, and everyone stood ready for instant action the moment he sang out, "There she blows!" Then it came, a great full-throated shout: *"There she blows! There—there!"*

"Where away?" the captain shouted.

"Off the starboard bow, three points!"

"How far?"

"Two miles!" The lookout was shouting like a maniac. The entire crew were shouting like maniacs. The captain shouted, "Boats!" In an instant three whaleboats were lowered from their davits and filled with five men apiece. Only the cook and cooper were left on board as "ship keepers."

Paul manned an oar in the third boat steered by the second mate, who roared encouragement to the rowers as he sat by the long, heavy steering oar. The harpooner, pulling on his oar in the bow, also shouted encouragement. The rest just rowed with all their strength. Suddenly the mate picked up the harpoon line and wound it several times around the vertical wooden drum fixed astern. He raised his arm for silence and signaled the harpooner, "Up with you. Let her have it!"

The harpooner dropped his oar, snatched the harpoon from its bracket, raised it with both hands above his head, and hurled it with all his might a little behind the whale's eye. The boat lurched as the harpoon thrust deep and true. The mate yelled, "Back, boys! Back her hard!" The sea churned and heaved. A hundred fathom of line whipped out of the tub stowed in the stern. Uncoiling in a single smoking minute, it shot hissing like a deadly snake across the oars.

"Wet the line! wet the line!" the mate yelled to the tub oarsman as the others backed water but the whale was now towing the boat. The mate tried to brake the line as they sped through the boiling sea. Then to Paul's astonishment, the mate and the harpooner changed places, so that when the whale tired, the mate could thrust the long, razor-sharp spear into its vitals for the final blow. The harpooner was now the "boat steerer," and the mate was yelling for them to haul away at the line.

The boat neared the whale again. The mate leaned forward and thrust his spear deep into the whale near its eye. "Back her, lads!" he ordered, and the boat shot off just as the mammoth flukes lifted and beat the sea into reddened foam around them. The men stared in fascinated, fearful awe as the great whale rolled and writhed. Then with a deep, agonized, bellowing groan it "blew its blood."

The red fountain of the whale's death rained over the excited men baptizing in blood the exaltation of their murder lust. Everything had gone perfectly. The whale was dead, and everyone else was alive and intact.

3

Revolution

It had been a thoroughly satisfying hunt. The satiated men rowed back to the ship, seeing the dead whale they towed behind them as money already jingling in their pockets. Every boat had killed a whale. Soon the hold would be stacked high with barrels and barrels of high-priced oil.

They lashed their sperm whale to the starboard side of the ship, the tail toward the bow. Between its eye and flipper, they bored a hole for an enormous hook secured by tackle to the mast. The carpenter made a wooden scaffold to hang over the ship's side for a few of the crew to stand on for the flensing—stripping the blubber from the carcass.

They began to cut at the head with razor-edged knives on long pole handles. Long, foot-thick strips of blubber were peeled off from nose to tail and hauled aboard with block, tackle, and windlass. Even on a calm day, it took five hours to get the whale aboard piecemeal. On a wind-tossed sea, flensing was a long, dangerous job, and many men ended it under the waves.

Once on board the blubber was cut into square blocks and then into slices called "Bible leaves," which were fed to the tryworks to melt down in the huge iron pot. The fire in the brick furnace was started by wood, then stoked with the "crackling" or residue left in the pot after the oil had been rendered out. Slipping and sliding on the slimy, blood-soaked deck, the exhausted men worked in the sickening stench day and night for over fifty hours, until all the blubber had been cut up and boiled and the stripped carcass cut free of the ship.

Paul didn't mind hard work, but he had chosen the sea because he wished to be a "marineer," not a butcher in a slaughterhouse. Whaling ships were good schools, but his apprenticeship was over. He wasn't a learner any longer. He was a seaman. He would continue to sail on the high seas but not after whales.

Sailing home from the whaling ground, Paul studied all he could learn about navigation. He kept a sharp lookout to familiarize himself with the navigational hazards of the Gulf and Caribbean. "There were always three things that I paid attention to," he said later, "latitude, lead, and lookout." The lead was needed near home. They hit fog and had to make a landing in New Bedford, sounding with the lead as they went, to check the water's depth. They nearly grounded at the river's mouth, until the pilot came aboard and guided the ship into harbor.

The pilot gave them their first news. After the Boston Tea Party, the British had passed a restraining act to punish the recalcitrant Massachusetts capital. New Englanders were now barred from the North Atlantic whaling grounds, where they competed with English whaling vessels. Any ship that wished to go whaling someplace else needed to obtain a permit and post a £2,000 bond.

Paul's captain was enraged at this latest harassment. He and the other Nantucket whaling captains made it a practice to follow the whale's annual North Atlantic migrations. They fitted out their ships during the winter, sailed south to the Gulf or Caribbean in the spring to take their catch, then refitted and sailed north again. The re-

strictive legislation made all this impossible. But the restraining act was a reprieve for Paul, for it meant that
ships that had been used for whaling would have to transfer to the carrying trade.

Indeed, once back in New Bedford, Paul was able to
sign on immediately as a common hand on board a general
cargo vessel carrying codfish to the West Indies in return
for salt and molasses. This second voyage was also edu-
cational. This time he learned from the West Indies what
it meant to be a slave.

The West Indies produced sugar, and the large sugarcane plantations of the "Sugar Islands" demanded large
numbers of slaves. The Indians of the Caribbean could not
be enslaved. They died instead. So, slaves were sought in
Africa. Trading posts were established on the West African coast. But as one trader remarked: "The blacks were
so wilful and loth to leave their own country, that they
have often leap'd out of the canoes, boat and ship, into
the sea, and kept under water til they were drowned."
Some jumped into the mouths of hungry sharks to escape
enslavement.

Slave-ship captains didn't like losing part of their
cargo before they even set sail. They expected the trader
to pack the ship tightly, for more slaves meant more
profit. So slaves were branded like cattle and shipped to
the Indies like logwood. Cattle could not have survived
in the filthy, dark, stinking holds of slave ships, where
the blacks were stacked in three layers and allowed only
enough space to lie chained flat on their backs.

One out of every eight slaves died before reaching
the Indies, either from disease, starvation, or despair.
They committed suicide the only way they could—by
swallowing their own tongues. So many black corpses
were tossed overboard that slave ships were invariably
trailed by man-eating sharks. But the lives lost subtracted
little from the slavers' enormous profits. There were

always eager buyers for the "black gold" of the Indies—especially in America.

The islands "seasoned" the slaves. They were either worked to death, in four or five years, or resold, well broken in, to the American colonies. Mainland planters preferred "seasoned" slaves to the raw product fresh from the wilds of Africa. Slaves were seldom freed. It might set a bad example for the other "work units" and lead them to believe themselves human. It was this brutal, dehumanizing "seasoning" that so appalled Paul.

So many slaves were brought to the islands from Africa that it was far cheaper to buy new workers than to breed, feed, or keep any alive. The plantation owners, most of whom lived far away in England, wanted only productivity and profits. So the job of the plantation overseer was to produce a lot of sugar as cheaply as possible. No time or land was wasted on growing food. Slaves were worked from sunup to sundown, with thirty minutes off to eat their one daily meal of a pint of grain and half a fish—usually rotten because it was shipped in from New England.

Women had to do the same work at the same pace as the men. Pregnant women had to work up to the time of childbirth. If they fell behind the other workers, they were whipped. Women carried their babies on their backs in the fields. If they stopped working to feed them, they were whipped. Whips were made of plaited cowhide and made wounds so large a man's finger could be inserted in them. The men were often punished by being suspended to a tree with iron weights tied around their necks and waists, or their ears were cropped and their limbs broken.

His voyage to the Indies also seasoned Paul. He never wanted to view those islands again. The next island he was to spend some time on was the war-surrounded island of Manhattan. At sea Paul had heard nothing about war, but once they docked in New Bedford, he heard of nothing else.

While he was at sea, the Massachusetts Provincial Congress decided to counter British harassment with preparations for war. General Thomas Gage, Massachusetts' military governor, decided to counter the rebels' amassing of military supplies with a surprise attack at the supply depot in Concord. But Paul Revere and William Dawes alerted the countryside, and the aroused minutemen fought the British at Lexington and Concord, drove them back to Boston, and surrounded the city. The Second Continental Congress in Philadelphia resolved to make the conflict a countrywide affair and named Virginian George Washington commander in chief of the Continental forces. After the battle of Bunker Hill, the British evacuated Boston and sailed for Halifax.

Paul learned that blacks had fought and died with the Massachusetts militia at Lexington and Concord, and two months later at Bunker Hill. Two of the heroes of the Bunker Hill battle were black. Peter Salem, who had been a slave in Framingham, Massachusetts, won the admiration of his fellow soldiers by shooting the British Major John Pitcairn. And Salem Poor won the praise of all his superiors, who said that at Bunker Hill he "behaved like an experienced officer as well as an excellent soldier." In an official commendation presented to the Massachusetts General Court, Salem Poor's officers said: "We would only beg leave to say, in the person of this said negro centres a brave and gallant soldier. The reward to so great and distinguished a character, we submit to the Congress."

Paul was not surprised to learn of their bravery. Blacks had fought well for Massachusetts in the French and Indian Wars, too—even though as early as 1656 the colonists had excluded blacks from militia service, for fear they would use their guns against their masters. So Paul was not surprised either at the news that, despite the bravery of the blacks in battle, General Washington's army was officially excluding all Negro soldiers.

The Continental Congress had made the decision. The new Continental Army represented all the colonies, so it had to be responsive to the requirements of them all —south as well as north. After King George III had proclaimed the American colonies to be in open rebellion, the same Continental Congress proclaimed a Declaration of Independence. But the slaves remained enslaved.

Paul knew that, even in the North, the blacks were too different in color and culture to be thought of always as people. After all, unlike the Indians, they had allowed themselves to be enslaved. The New Englanders thought of slaves mainly as a commodity to be shipped from Africa to the West Indies or the southern colonies. A few slaves were brought back to New England, where the Puritans called them "servants," but they controlled them by slave codes.

Because there were so few slaves in New England, there was no fear of a slave revolt. So the slave codes were far less harsh than elsewhere. In Massachusetts slaves had a few legal rights. And they were taught trades, because there was only a demand for skilled labor. Small-farm Massachusetts had no plantations. And since some Puritans wanted to convert their slaves, which meant they had to read the Bible, many slaves were taught to read and write.

Only the Quakers spoke out against slavery. As early as 1688, they drafted a formal protest against "the traffic of men-body." By 1776 American Quakers had not only disavowed slavery but had also set up schools to prepare slaves for freedom by teaching them how to read and write. The Nantucket Quakers Paul knew were the only whites he wished to work for. He respected them and their principles. They supported neither Britain nor the former colonies in this new war because their "religion would not admit of their taking up arms in a military way in any case whatever." So Paul decided to side with them.

The Quaker Nantucket captains just wanted to sail their ships in peace. But neither side would let them. America was converting fishing vessels into armed ships, and Britain, after blockading the American coast to close the colonies to all commerce, singled out the Nantucket whaling fleet for destruction. Swooping down on the un-armed whalers, the Royal Navy either seized them as war booty or sank or burned them.

The Nantucket captains had a difficult choice: stay ashore and starve or make a voyage and risk capture or sinking. They chose to sail, and Paul sailed with them. His voyage lasted three days. On the third day, the ship was captured by a blockading frigate. According to the provisions of the hated restraining act, any prisoners taken on board an American vessel could be compelled, without distinction of rank, to serve as common seamen on a King's ship.

Paul's captain was asked by his captors which would he choose—imprisonment or the forecastle of a British man-of-war. Having had enough of the British and their "legal" piracy, he retorted, "Hang me if you will to the yardarm of your ship, but do not ask me to be a traitor to my country!"

The British, who respected that kind of answer, did neither. They took him and his crew and imprisoned them all in New York City.

General William Howe had just captured the city, which was to remain the British base of operations throughout the war. But on September 21, shortly after the occupation, a fire destroyed almost three hundred of the city's buildings. With his troops wintering in the houses that remained, Howe had no space for new prisoners. So Paul and his comrades were soon freed.

4

Privateers,Pirates, and Petitions

Paul Cuffe returned to his Westport, Massachusetts, farm. The war had started in Massachusetts, but by 1777 it was being fought elsewhere—in New Jersey, Pennsylvania, and New York. General "Gentleman Johnny" Burgoyne had assured Britain that he and his Indian and Loyalist allies would split the colonies apart along the Hudson River.

News of raids and rumors of atrocities in the Mohawk Valley sped through New England. Militiamen flocked to halt Burgoyne. Finally, at Saratoga, surrounded by a force three times his own, Burgoyne surrendered. But the Indians and Loyalist rangers continued their raids on the isolated settlements around the Mohawk Valley. In Massachusetts, all Indians soon became somewhat suspect.

Paul began to feel uncomfortable on his Westport farm. Some Massachusetts men had even begun to question the loyalty of the blacks. After the Continental Congress had barred them from the army, the British declared all Negroes "free, that are able and willing to bear arms, they joining his Majesty's troops, as soon as may be." Many blacks did join the British and were used as military laborers, spies, guides, and informers. The British were especially eager to recruit black sailors as pilots for the King's ships in American coastal waters.

Paul decided to go back to sea but not on an armed ship. By this time the British blockade was so effective that all the Nantucket whaling ships had been sent into the West Indies trade. The mainland ports had turned chiefly to privateering. Since 1776 Congress had authorized the arming of private ships as privateers to sail against the commercial and war ships of Britain. Privateering became very popular. It was much more profitable than fishing or trading, and a far more effective armed force against the British than the infant American navy, which was too weak to operate as a fleet.

The pacifist Quakers of Nantucket refused to be privateers, but they were willing to fight back if a blockader tried to capture their ship. One sloop had two captains aboard when the British tried boarding her. The first captain, armed with a handspike, knocked the British seamen down right and left while the second captain grabbed their commander and held him headforemost over the ship's quarter until he begged for his life and surrendered. When the Quaker captains turned their prisoners over to the American authorities, they were asked: "Why didn't you drop overboard that fellow you held so long over the quarter?" The second captain replied with embarrassment: "Friend, we had lost our boats, and I was afraid he would drown."

Paul would only ship with the Nantucket Quakers, so he had no choice but to sail again to the West Indies. While he was away, the British dispatched a punitive expedition against the privateer ports. A fleet of a dozen ships-of-war and six transports was ordered to burn out the "rebel nests of privateers" and get supplies to feed the King's troops in New York.

They sailed up the Connecticut and Massachusetts coast and anchored in Clark's Cove. Waiting for nightfall, they made a bridge of boats for two thousand men to cross by moonlight to the shore. But the inhabitants of

New Bedford were not taken by surprise. As the British marched through the countryside, the alarm guns were sounded, and the population of New Bedford fled, leaving their homes and ships to the invaders.

For several hours the redcoats plundered and looted the town. They burned the houses, the cooper shops, warehouses, ropewalks, blacksmith shops, and the candle house. With the town burning behind them, they went to the harbor and burned all the ships anchored there. A number of vessels were destroyed, including one snow, one bark, six brigs, five schooners, and eight sloops. After the war, it took New Bedford five years to recover as a port. Not only were all the ships, shops, and houses burned, but the whaling gear and all the supplies stored in the warehouses were also destroyed.

The British raiding fleet then crossed Buzzards Bay, stripping Naushon and Nonannesset, two of the Elizabeth Islands, on their way to strip Martha's Vineyard of all its sheep, ships, cattle, and money. Nantucket was next on the list, but an east-northeast gale blew up, and the fleet could not beat up against it in the narrow confines of the sound. The gale blew for three days and nights. Packed aboard the ships, the plundered sheep and cattle moaned, and the stale air stank with their stench. The British gave up and returned to New York.

Nantucket was saved, and Paul's captain still had a port to come home to. But Paul couldn't ship out of New Bedford again. The privateers couldn't either, and the Royal Navy now dominated the waters of Buzzards Bay. A British raiding party had also ravaged the Connecticut shore of Long Island Sound to prevent privateers from using the ports there. And Narragansett Bay was closed to privateers with the British in Newport at the bay's entrance.

Paul realized that, with the British controlling the two bays and the Sound, the little fishing and farming communities on their shores would be dependent for supplies on any coastal trading ships that could sail past the blockading frigates. So Paul and his brother David built a small open boat. Only such a diminutive craft could slip in and out of the coastal coves unnoticed by the British gunboats stationed offshore.

With his new boat the twenty-year-old Paul Cuffe went into business with his brother as a blockade-running coaster. The coastal settlements on Buzzards Bay, Narragansett Bay, and the Sound were so eager for supplies that any trader was well paid for whatever goods he could sneak through the blockade. Paul knew his home waters well, and he prospered.

Unfortunately others, who were not interested in trade, also knew the hidden bays and inlets of Paul's home coastline. The area was infested with pirates looking for plunder. Paul was attacked often. Sometimes he lost his boat as well as his cargo. His brother David found the shipping business too risky and returned to his farm. But Paul persevered. Whenever a voyage was successful, he put all the profits into building a better boat. Within a year he had expanded to a fifteen-ton closed-deck vessel, *Box Iron.*

At sea Paul dodged the frigates and fended off the pirates for free enterprise. On land he fought to be free of discrimination. He spent most of the winter of 1780 on land. It was one of the worst winters New Englanders had ever experienced. All the coves and inlets were frozen solid. Even Nantucket Island was surrounded by ice. In Morristown, New Jersey, Washington's army mutinied under conditions more severe than their painful 1778 winter at Valley Forge.

As he could not sail, it seemed to Paul a good time to petition Massachusetts for a small portion of the political equality the colony was fighting to win from Britain. Massachusetts was so sure its cause would triumph that it had just ratified a constitution. The new constitution abolished slavery by stating that "all men are born free and equal." Paul wanted the constitution's elaborate safeguards protecting the individual extended to protect the blacks and Indians, too.

"No Taxation Without Representation" had been an early battle cry in the struggle for independence. Paul now decided to fight with Massachusetts over the same issue. The commonwealth did not allow blacks or Indians to vote, but did require them to pay poll taxes and property taxes if they owned land. Paul protested by petition.

Individual blacks, for several years, had been petitioning the General Court of Massachusetts for their freedom and winning. In 1773 a group of slaves had petitioned the Massachusetts legislature, saying: "We have no property! we have no wives! we have no children! no city! no country!" The next year another slave group petitioned, stating that, in common with other men, they had a right to their freedom. But the Massachusetts assembly had turned them down. It realized that the freeing of individual blacks, one at a time, was quite different from freeing groups of slaves by an assembly act that might establish a broad principle of universal freedom.

It was precisely to establish such a principle that Paul decided to submit his petition. He asked the legislature to exempt from taxation all who were denied their citizenship rights. If they were not allowed to vote, then they shouldn't have to pay taxes. If they possessed property, then, by the new Massachusetts constitution, they were qualified to vote and hold public office. The petition was addressed to "The Honorable Council and House of Representatives, in General Court Assembled, for the State of Massachusetts Bay in New England" on February 10, 1780.

The petition of several poor Negroes and mulattoes who are inhabitants of the town of Dartmouth humbly showeth that we being chiefly of the African extract, and by reason of long bondage and hard slavery, we have been deprived of enjoying the profits of our labor or the advantages of inheriting estates from our parents, as our neighbors the white people do, having some of us not long enjoyed our own freedom; yet of late, contrary to the invariable customs and practice of the country, we have been, and now are, taxed both in our polls and that small pittance of estate which, through much hard labor and industry, we have got together to sustain ourselves and families withall. We apprehend it, therefore, to be hard usage, and will doubtless (if continued) reduce us to a state of beggary, whereby we shall become a burthen to others, if not timely prevented by the interposition of your justice and power.

Your petitioners further show, that we apprehend ourselves to be aggrieved, in that, while we are not allowed the privilege of freemen of the state, having no vote or influence in the election of those that tax us, yet many of our color (as is well known) have cheerfully entered the field of battle in the defence of the common cause, and that (as we conceive) against a similar exertion of power (in regard to taxation), too well known to need a recital in this place.

That these the most honorable court, we humbly beseech they would take this into consideration and let us aside from paying tax or taxes for we are not allowed to vote in the town meetings or to choose an officer. Neither are the poor despised miserable Black people ever heard in the active court of the General Assembly. And we have not an equal chance with white people neither by sea nor by land. We pray that those who have the rule in their hands may be merciful unto the poor and needy. We most humbly request, therefore, that you will, in your wisdom

40

and power, grant us relief from taxation while under our present depressed circumstances.

The petition was signed by Paul Cuffe, his brother John, and five of their neighbors. Adventur Child and Pero Coggeshall signed their names, but Samuel Gray, Pero Howland and Pero Russell had to sign with "X (his mark)."

The petition was rejected, as were all the other petitions that Paul submitted to the authorities. And the Cuffe brothers noted these rejections: "This is the copy of the petitions which we did deliver unto the honorable council and house for relief from taxation in the days of our distress. But we received none." So they backed their words with deeds. To protest the discrimination, Paul and his brother John refused to pay their county property taxes and poll taxes.

The authorities answered this defiance with a warrant for their arrest. At their trial they requested relief from taxation since they were "Indian men and by law not the subjects of taxation for any estate, real or personal, and humbly pray your Honors that, as they are assessed jointly a double poll tax and the said Paul is a minor for whom the said John is not by law answerable or chargeable, that the said poll taxes aforesaid, may be abated to them and they allowed their reasonable costs."

But the court declared them guilty. They paid their taxes. Paul Cuffe's fight for civil rights was finished. But his desire for it was not.

5

Shipping

The year 1783 brought peace to the new United States of America and a wife to Paul Cuffe. Her name was Alice Pequit. She was a member of his mother's tribe of Wampanoag Indians. Paul now worked even harder than he had before. For the end of the war also brought the end of the British blockade and the end of their hated navigation acts. The northern fishing grounds off Newfoundland and Nova Scotia were open again.

Many of the older Nantucketers, who had retired from whaling, went north to fish for cod. Codfishing had been so successful during the war that they continued it. Paul sailed with them to the codfish banks off Nova Scotia on his new eighteen-ton schooner. Then the British closed the main market for cod by banning all imports from the United States into the West Indies.

But the Massachusetts sea captains didn't care. They had all gone a-whaling. With no hunters for so long, the whales had multiplied in all the old whaling grounds. Every ship returned to port with her hold full of whale oil. Paul, who had stayed home, went back to his local coastal trading business. With the competition out hunting whales, he did very well.

New Bedford became a whaling port again. And Paul got a twenty-five-ton schooner. He named her the *Sun Fish* after the first fish caught from her deck. The *Sun Fish* was large enough to require another hand. So Paul asked his Indian brother-in-law, Michael Wainer, who was a good seaman, to help him sail her. They carried anything and everything, and sailed in whatever direction business prospects suggested.

Then with so much whale oil pouring in, the whale market became flooded. Prices fell rapidly. Britain tried to protect her whaling industry by placing an import duty of £18 per ton on the oil of other countries. With their best market walled off by a duty, whalers tried to sell all their oil in America. But Americans had gotten used to tallow candles during the war, when there was no whale oil, and saw no reason to pay more for the better light of spermaceti candles.

As depression struck, the shipping industry demanded action from their new government. Congress tried to pass an American navigation act to counter Britain's navigation laws. But the central government had no power over the quarreling states who could agree on nothing except their own sovereignty. John Adams went to London, but could obtain no commercial concessions from the British. "If the United States wishes to make a trade treaty," the British Foreign Minister said, "they ought properly to send over thirteen representatives, as there is no sign of unity at home."

The depression deepened. In Massachusetts the farmers rebelled under the leadership of Daniel Shays, an ex-captain in Washington's army. Jefferson said he liked "a little rebellion now and then." But Massachusetts didn't. The state crushed Shays's rebellion, and passed a navigation act of its own restricting trade with Britain. Businessmen talked of establishing a monarchy as America's only defense against chaos. But Massachusetts Congressman Fisher Ames said:

Monarchy is like a full-rigged ship, trim and beautiful, with all hands at their stations and the captain at the helm. It excutes its maneuvers sharply and operates with the greatest efficiency, but if it hits a rock, the frail hull is crushed and the vessel sinks. Democracy is like a raft—hard to navigate, impossible to keep on course, and distressingly slow. If it runs onto a rock, it simply careens off and takes a new course. But if it has the virtue of always staying afloat, it has disadvantages, too. Your feet are wet all the time.

The Nantucketers grew desperate. Whaling was Nantucket's only industry. A group of islanders moved to Nova Scotia and others were preparing to leave. So William Rotch, Nantucket's greatest whale-oil merchant, took charge. Rotch was "much esteemed by the people for his knowledge, prudence, and integrity. He appeared to be as a prince on the island." Rotch believed that the whaling industry should be a world commodity as long as there were Nantucket men to supply officers and men for a fleet. He regarded the supplying of whale oil to the great cities of the world, for the "light of progress," as a world public utility that should belong to no political regime. It should be international and answerable only to the dictates of supply and demand.

But the nation's statesmen did not seem ready for world leadership. They were unable to return the world's commerce to a logical balance. They could not see beyond the narrow confines of tariff boundaries, and visualize world trade as a common marketplace for the people of the world to trade freely for the advantage of all. So it was up to the practical merchants to show the way. Rotch's brother-in-law had established a Nantucket colony in Nova Scotia, where whale oil could be exported duty-free to England. Rotch would establish one in France.

He left the Nantucket firm of William Rotch and Sons in the hands of his son-in-law, and sent his son William, Jr., to New Bedford. His father, the cofounder of New Bedford, had recently died, having never recovered from the British destruction of his town. William, Jr., worked hard to rebuild the New Bedford whaling fleet and increase America's consumption of whale oil for street lighting, machinery, and lamps. And he succeeded, aided by America's increased stability and prosperity after a new strong Constitution was ratified that shifted the authority and power from the separate states to the people.

Paul Cuffe did not place his trust in a constitution that excluded Indians and counted a slave as three fifths of a man. The new Constitution for a democratic republic rested upon the dominion of property with no guarantees of human liberties. Paul Cuffe preferred to place his trust in William Rotch, Jr.

Under his care, the port of New Bedford grew and prospered, as did the business enterprises of Paul Cuffe. Rotch took a great interest in Cuffe's affairs. He frequently employed him to transport lumber, food supplies, and general merchandise from New Bedford to Martha's Vineyard and Nantucket. Cuffe considered Rotch his leading counselor and protector, and usually consulted with him first before starting any major venture.

It was undoubtedly Rotch's influence upon Paul Cuffe that caused Cuffe to embark in 1793 on a whaling expedition. He sailed on his new forty-two-ton schooner, *Mary*. Paul's wife's name was Alice, but his sister and daughter were named Mary. Paul and his brother-in-law, Michael Wainer, sailed with a crew of ten relatives and friends to the Strait of Belle Isle whaling grounds between Labrador and Newfoundland.

They left New Bedford in early April, sailing northeast past Nova Scotia to the Grand Banks, where the cold Labrador current met the warm Gulf Stream, causing thick fog. When the fog lifted a little, they saw "several ice islands of divers shapes" carried down by the Labrador current. Cuffe brought the ship to, "under a trisail and foresail not daring to run we knew not whither among ye ice and fog. The weather is freezing cold; nights short; sea rolling and tumbling. It snowed so thick we had to clear the deck of snow almost overshoes deep."

The crew killed seabirds called "heights" and made meat pies to vary the shipboard fare. "Our cabin our delight, the fire pleasant, our allowance to every man on board his belly-full and more too if he wants." Then a hard heavy gale blew up and raised a very long high sea, "a right top gallant swell. We lay to under a trisail and let her drive and she lay very well and made good weather of it. But we were very uneasy for fear of driving amongst the ice."

Sudden storms were common in the strait, and the gale blew them to the whaling ground already occupied by four fully equipped whaling ships. Paul's ship only had two harpoon boats, one of which was too old to be of much use. After one look at Captain Cuffe and his crew, the other whaling captains decided that the cooperative business of whaling was not cooperative enough to include the black *Mary*.

That left Paul with two choices. He could either sail home or whale alone. The other captains naturally expected Captain Cuffe to go home, whaling being too dangerous to try alone. But Paul refused to leave. If he were afraid to tackle dangerous undertakings alone, he would still be on the farm with brother John.

The other captains were appalled when they saw Captain Cuffe starting to launch his harpoon boats. His inexperienced crew would frighten and drive the whales away from everyone's reach. The captains would have to forget their prejudice and cooperate or all the ships might return home with empty holds.

To prove their worth, Paul and his men had to be better whalers than the other crews. And they were! The entire fleet killed seven whales. Six of the seven were caught by Paul's crew. Two were killed by Paul himself. An equal division of the kill filled every ship full of whale oil and bone. Paul turned his proceeds into a new schooner—the sixty-nine ton *Ranger*.

But he did not sail the *Ranger* to the British-controlled northern whaling grounds. France had declared war on Britain, and Washington issued a neutrality proc-·lamation. Britain answered with Orders in Council, interfering with neutral shipping, which meant the seizure of American ships and the imprisonment or impressment of American crews.

Paul Cuffe went back to coastal shipping. Having conquered Yankee prejudice with profits and excellence, Cuffe and his crew sailed south on the *Ranger* to test the Maryland market. Learning that there was a reasonably priced cargo of corn available in Vienna, Maryland, Paul sailed up the Nanticoke River to this tiny backwater community.

His arrival caused great "astonishment and alarm." The townsfolk surmised that Cuffe and his crew must be a band of escaped slaves who had stolen a ship, turned pirate, and were coming to Vienna to lead a slave revolt. He was refused a landing permit until he patiently proved his papers to be in order. Having legally won the right to be in Vienna, Paul and his crew next had to win over the citizenry by being more white than the whites. They were so successful that in a few days the only color noticed in Vienna was the color of Cuffe's money.

Cuffe's trade with Vienna proved advantageous enough to both sides for him to return for a second shipment of corn. The two voyages yielded him a $2,000 profit which, as usual, he invested. But this time the investment was in land, not ships. For not only were the British making shipping difficult, but France had also started an undeclared naval war on the United States.

France was angry, because, after helping America win her revolution, America refused to help France in her war with England. The Democrats wanted to help France. The Federalists did not. So when Federalist John Adams became President, he repudiated the "Franklin Treaty" of 1778 that guaranteed American aid in French wars in return for French aid during the War of Independence. In retaliation France ordered the seizure of American ships. Many whaleships were captured, and Nantucket lost a million dollars in a war that was never declared.

Paul Cuffe preferred to remain on land during any war, declared or undeclared. He bought a large $3,500 farm in Westport, Massachusetts, on the shore of the Westport River. Here he had direct access to the sea. Cuttyhunk Island, the home of his Wampanoag relatives, was just a short sail across Buzzards Bay, and New Bedford was not much farther up the coast.

Cuffe built a wharf and a warehouse on his new land. Now he could oversee his shipbuilding, trading, and farming ventures from home. He could spend more time with his wife of fourteen years, and more closely supervise the rearing of his two sons and five daughters. He wanted them to have the formal education he lacked. But there was no school anywhere in Westport.

Believing in direct action as a solution for any problem, Paul Cuffe met with the townsmen and farmers of

Westport. He spoke of the community's need for a school and urged immediate action. Nothing was done. The people of Westport preferred not to spend their money for a nonsegregated school.

So Cuffe spent his. He built a schoolhouse on his own land for his children. Then he offered free use of the school to all Westport children. It was too good a bargain for his thrifty Yankee neighbors to refuse. Paul Cuffe's school remained the town's only school for many years. And Westport was the first community in America with integrated schooling.

6

Sierra Leone

Now in his middle years in the midst of his Westport holdings, Paul Cuffe could have been a comfortably wealthy, courtly, portly country squire. In America where one's financial standing to some extent determines one's social standing, the sober, industrious, civic-minded Cuffe, with his country estate and fleet of ships, should have ranked high in his community. He dressed elegantly and spoke elegantly, but he was not colored elegantly.

The only whites who had ever regarded Paul Cuffe as a person rather than as a curiosity were the Nantucket-born Quakers in New Bedford. Most of the business leaders along the Buzzards Bay coast of southeastern Massachusetts were Quakers, and all their social activities were meeting oriented. The Quakers preached the spiritual equality of all men and actively urged the abolition of slavery.

But Paul Cuffe knew that being against slavery was not the same as being for the blacks. Many Quaker Meetings refused to admit blacks as members, and others segregated them on separate benches. The Westport Meeting had no black members. Cuffe would be the first. Therefore he was determined not to join until his wealth had bought him enough respect to be welcomed as an equal by the Westport Quakers.

Paul Cuffe formally joined the Westport Quaker Meeting in 1808. He was not seeking social acceptance. That was impossible in the America of 1808. Blacks were scarcely noticed by whites until they commanded attention by climbing the highest peaks in the business and financial world. Cuffe had finally scaled those heights. He was America's first wealthy black man, and the first to captain his own ships.

It was not enough. He had not struggled to climb so far merely to be noticed. He wanted equality. But he realized that equality for himself was meaningless without equality for his people as well. Even a small portion of political equality was beyond his reach, although he had fought very hard for it. The Quakers, as a group, had already accomplished far more than he alone could ever hope to do.

They had organized antislavery societies in every state from Massachusetts to Virginia. The societies had worked hard to abolish slavery in the North and prohibit the African slave trade. Paul Cuffe visited the societies and met many distinguished, dedicated men who welcomed him as an associate. But it was not enough. Paul was not a participant. He was a crusader.

The Quakers did good work, but groups moved too slowly. Too much needed to be done. Paul Cuffe was forty-nine years old. He would only be able to cushion his children with his wealth for a few more years. When they left home, he could no longer protect them from the soul-searing discrimination of a slave-owning America. He had only been able to find the equality he sought on board his own ship. But his children could not live in the middle of the sea. For them and for the rest of his people, a new land was needed.

America no longer belonged to his mother's people,

and it wanted his father's people only as slaves. Back in Africa, everyone was black. If he could find a part of Africa that rejected the slave trade and make it as economically self-sufficient as his farm, then *that* would be a good land for his people.

For the next few years Paul Cuffe tried to discover all he could about Africa from Quaker groups interested in the redemption of the Dark Continent. At the same time, he increased his fleet of ships with the 162-ton bark *Hero,* the 268-ton sloop *Alpha,* and his favorite, the 109-ton brig *Traveller.* He wanted to be able to move just as soon as he found a suitable location.

Then he learned about Sierra Leone—the "Mountain of the Lion." The colony was on the coast of the Nantucketers' whaling ground in the Guinea Basin. Located at the mouth of the Sierra Leone River, it lay in the westernmost part of Africa—"the bulge"—midway between his father's birthplace in Ghana and the Bissagos Islands (off present-day Guinea-Bissau), the home of the best all-around African whalemen. The Sierra Leone estuary was once the haunt of slavers and privates, but the British got rid of them when a colony was established in 1787.

It was because of this colony that Paul Cuffe chose Sierra Leone. It had been established by the British Quakers for former American slaves as a democratic, self-governing, prosperous African Negro state. It seemed very much like what he wanted to create. It could be the answer to his dream—except that it had no history of success.

After the American Revolution all the slaves who had been promised freedom for fighting for the British were sent to Nova Scotia—to starve. A few managed to reach England, where some stranded black sailors joined them in their poverty. The Quakers noticed the wretchedness and suffering of the American blacks and tried to collect funds for them as a Committee for the Black Poor. But the

British did not want to feed them—they just wanted to get rid of them.

An unemployed amateur botanist, Henry "Flycatcher" Smeathman, then contacted the committee. He had lived for three years on the Banana Islands just off the southern end of the Sierra Leone Peninsula on the west coast of Africa. The island, where he had lived and gathered specimens for London's Kew Gardens, belonged to the Caulkers family, who were descended from an English trader and the daughter of an African chief.

Smeathman the Flycatcher offered to remove all of London's black poor and establish them in a colony on the Sierra Leone Peninsula. He assured the members of the committee that, if they gave him £4 per head for re-location expenses, their investment would be returned many times over within a few years, because the Sierra Leone climate and soil were perfect for a commercially profitable plantation economy.

Impressed with his arguments, the committee asked the British Treasury to subsidize Smeathman's scheme. The treasury agreed if the committee guaranteed the removal of all the blacks and managed their colony in Sierra Leone. No one remembered that the Flycatcher had, just the year before, advised the British government against establishing a prison colony in West Africa because it was unhealthy. They thought only of his promise of riches through trade and agriculture.

Just before the blacks were to leave to populate the Flycatcher's dream of a domain like the Caulkers-controlled Banana Islands, Smeathman died of a "putrid fever." So Granville Sharp, the noted British champion of Negro rights, took charge and induced the Royal Navy to provide Captain Thompson's *Nautilus* to transport the blacks. But he couldn't get many to agree to be taken to his African "Province of Freedom."

Sharp was undaunted. The British government had

kept its end of the bargain, and he intended the committee to keep its as well. He had the London authorities round up for deportation any Negro indigent found in the streets. They found four hundred. And while they were cleaning up the streets, they got sixty white prostitutes to ship off as well. The committee saw the emigrants off on April 8, 1787, with high hopes for the money-making potential of the new colony.

They were disappointed. Captain Thompson purchased twenty-seven square miles on the north shore of the Sierra Leone Peninsula from King Tom, the local Temne chief. The colony cost £59 worth of arms, ammunition, cotton cloth, metalware, tobacco, and rum. The settlers called their village Granville Town after Sharp. But the rains came before they could settle in permanently, and many died. Sharp "had but melancholy accounts of my poor little ill-thriven swarthy daughter, the unfortunate colony of Sierra Leone."

Two years later Granville Town was burned to the ground by King Jimmy, a local Temne subchief, in retaliation for the earlier burning of one of his towns by crewmen from a British warship. All who had not already become victims of the climate, the poor soil, and the hordes of malaria-bearing mosquitoes fled for their lives from Sharp's Province of Freedom. Alexander Falconbridge, a former slave-ship surgeon, collected forty-eight survivors and started another settlement two miles to the east along the Sierra Leone River. The new village of seventeen huts was controlled by a commercial company chartered by Parliament.

Many of the original colony's sponsors were directors of the new Sierra Leone Company. They still believed that the steamy tropical African territory with its limited natural resources would thrive. All the colony needed was a well-organized trading company to give it a more stable basis for development and a businessman chairman to replace Sharp and his dream of a self-governing colony. Then, with more emigrants, it would start returning profits to its investors.

The Sierra Leone Company sent Lieutenant Clarkson to Nova Scotia to remove twelve hundred more American Revolution blacks who were proving troublesome there. Clarkson brought them to the site of the original Sierra Leone settlement, which he renamed Freetown. The intensely religious, independent Nova Scotians respected the honest Clarkson, a religious man himself. He tried to persuade them to end their hatred and distrust of the whites and to trust the Sierra Leone Company.

But they had been cheated too often in the past. The blacks had no wish now to be governed by a company that had given them only five acres of poor land instead of the twenty of good land they had been promised. Still, they built their huts, cultivated their gardens, and raised hogs. They sent twelve fishing boats out daily and went to Gambia and Bance Island to trade for rum.

Then the Sierra Leone Company sent Dawes to replace Clarkson as governor. Dawes raised prices at the company store and watered the rum. The Nova Scotians threatened him with the fate of the recently guillotined Louis XVI. Dawes returned to England. Complete disaster struck when the French, at war with Britain, sailed into Freetown harbor in 1794, disguised as British men-of-war, and looted and destroyed everything they could find.

The Sierra Leone Company tried to recover from its financial setbacks by charging the Nova Scotians "quit-rents" to raise more revenue. The blacks refused to pay. The land, they said, had been promised to them "free of all expense." Finally, in 1800, charging that the company had not kept its promise about the land, the settlers rebelled. British troops put down the rebellion. The rebel leaders were executed and the rest were expelled from the colony.

This time the Sierra Leone Company repopulated their colony with 550 Maroons from Jamaica. The Maroons were slaves who had escaped into the deep valleys of the mountainous interior when the English drove the Spanish from Jamaica in 1660. They established an independent stronghold and fought the British troops to a standstill in the dense forests of their "Land of Look Behind"—so called because the British had to ride two men to a horse with one facing backward in case of an ambush. The Maroons won their bloody treaty of independence in 1739, but still waged a guerrilla war against the Jamaican planters and encouraged their slaves to escape.

The Maroons did not make the poor soil of Sierra Leone fruitful for the company, either. They refused even to go cultivate the fields, because of the constant threat of attack from the exiled rebels and their Temne allies. Moreover, all the cattle in Freetown had been slaughtered during the settlers' rebellion in order to feed the population. By 1802 it was clear that, without agricultural produce to export, the company could not succeed as a commercial venture.

The last of the company governors wrote that, considering all the unforeseen difficulties—from French invasion to settler rebellion and Temne attack—"the wonder is that the Colony exists rather than it has not flourished." For the Sierra Leone Company, their colony had become a bottomless pit into which immense sums of money disappeared without a trace. By 1807 the company was on the verge of bankruptcy. Parliament intervened. The company was relieved of its financial responsibility and allowed to transfer its rights to the Crown.

Sierra Leone became a crown colony in 1807, because the Crown had just declared the slave trade to be illegal. England's economy no longer rested on the products grown by slave labor in the Indies. Indies money had triggered the industrial revolution, and by 1807 England's economy was based on the export of manufactured goods made by English workers.

Freetown's harbor was needed as a naval base for the British warships that were being sent to protect British shipping and prevent slavers of any nation from carrying off slaves from West Africa. After all, if British traders were forbidden to deal in slaves, foreign slavers shouldn't be allowed to gain an advantage over them. All arrested slave ships were impounded and their slave cargo freed in Sierra Leone.

The black population of Freetown grew. But the British government and other whites left as soon as they could, calling the colony "the white man's grave." Thomas Thompson, the first crown colony governor, was a military man. He intended to turn the chaotic colony into an orderly and profitable agricultural enterprise. First he tidied up the streets by impounding all the free-roaming cattle. Next, he started the building of sounder government structures as symbols of his administration's permanency.

Then he tried to organize the independent Nova Scotians by drafting all adult males into a trained militia. It didn't work. The strong-willed Nova Scotians had no intention of changing their settled way of life and giving up their crafts and trade to work the unfertile soil of Sierra Leone. So Thompson turned to the numerous and more obedient survivors of the slave galleys whom Britain had freed and dumped on Sierra Leone's shore without a thought of how to feed them. Thompson settled them as a free peasantry in rural communities surrounding Freetown.

But before he had a chance to see if his scheme for increasing the agricultural productivity of Sierra Leone would work, he was recalled. He had found fault with his Sierra Leone Company predecessors and challenged the company's operations. The Quaker directors of the

Sierra Leone Company still controlled the colony. They had only relinquished to the Crown the burden and expense of governing and maintaining it.

They had not abandoned what they felt to be their moral obligation to the Negroes they had sent there. So they created the African Institution in 1807 to keep a watchful and beneficent eye on Sierra Leone. With the Duke of Gloucester, nephew and son-in-law of the King, as chairman of their influential board of directors, they were able to continue to wield considerable power over the administration and affairs of their former colony.

7

Eastward Bound

Paul Cuffe thought about the failure of Sierra Leone. Perhaps failure for the British would not be failure for him. He did not seek to make a profit. He only sought a self-sufficient settlement. Perhaps if a practical, independent black man whose motives were not mixed went to Sierra Leone and showed the settlers how to be self-sufficient, they might succeed. It certainly seemed worth trying.

Paul spoke to the American Quakers about his plans for Sierra Leone, and asked them to acquaint the British Quakers of the African Institution of his plans:

Esteemed Friends

I have for some years had it impressed on my mind to make a voyage to Sierra Leone in order to inspect the situation of the country. As I am of the African race I feel myself interested for them, and if I am favored with a talent I think I am willing that they should be benefitted thereby.

If you think it expedient to write to England to inform them that I have some concern in navigation, which if I concluded to settle there I would wish to

take with me so that the inhabitants might be benefitted both with agriculture and commerce; and that
in case I engage in the whale fishery whether I could
have encouragement such as bounty, or to carry the
productions of the country duty free to England.

If times should be so settled between this and next
fall so as to be advisable to undertake such a voyage,
it looks pretty clear to be put in execution in case
there should be encouragement.

I am your assured friend

Paul Cuffe

The influential members of the African Institution
were very interested in Cuffe's proposal. They wrote to
assure him that the institution would make every effort
to ensure the success of his contemplated voyage.

The American Quakers also urged him "to go forward
resolutely with his project." They knew that the nonslave-
owning whites were uncomfortable and a little fearful
of the Negro presence in America. The answer seemed to
be to return them to Africa. Thomas Jefferson, the declarer
of independence, said:

Nothing is more certainly written in the book of
fate than that these people [the blacks] are to be free;
nor is it less certain that the two races, equally free;
cannot live in the same government. Nature, habit,
opinion, have drawn indissoluble lines of distinction
between them. It is still in our power to direct the
process of emancipation and deportation, peaceably,
and in such slow degree, as the evil will wear off in-
sensibly, and their place be filled up by white laborers.

But every attempt to colonize Africa with American
free blacks had been rejected by the blacks themselves.

They were not going to move into the unknown for any white man's utopian promises. They knew nothing about this strange forbidding land that the whites fearfully called the Dark Continent.

The Quakers knew Paul Cuffe to be a sensible, determined man, who would always be careful to temper idealism with plenty of practicality. The blacks might have enough confidence in such a black leader to follow him to Africa. So many prominent Quakers provided him with letters of endorsement and recommendation. One was from a signer of the Declaration, America's foremost physician:

I have had the pleasure of a personal knowledge of Capt. Paul Cuffe for several years and from his conduct and conversation, as well as from the character I have uniformly heard of him from all who know him, I have been led to entertain a high opinion of his integrity and other moral virtues. He visits Sierra Leone in order to aid the benevolent views of the London African Institution toward the African nations. He is hereby recommended to the notice and protection of the friends of liberty, humanity, and Religion in every part of the world by

Philadelphia   Benjamin Rush, M.D.

President of the Society for abolishing the commerce in slaves, and for extending liberty to them.

Now all Cuffe had to do was sail to Sierra Leone and see for himself if the colony could be made economically self-sufficient. If it could, then Sierra Leone would be the new land of freedom and equality for black Americans.

On November 25, 1810, Paul Cuffe embarked on board his beloved brig *Traveller*. She slipped forth from her

Westport berth with her two tall masts proudly aloft. Her square sails filled as she tacked down the Westport River into Rhode Island Sound. Captain Cuffe pointed her bowsprit southwest toward Philadelphia and turned the helm over to his nephew, Thomas Wainer.

Michael Wainer, the Pequot Indian who had sailed so long with Cuffe after marrying Paul's sister Mary, had been replaced by his three sons. Thomas Wainer was master, John and Michael, Jr., were mates. The rest of the crew were six black friends from Westport: John Marsters, Samuel Hicks, Zachariah White, Joseph Hemmenway, Charles Freeling, and Thomas Caton.

The *Traveller* had been given a big send-off in Westport. The relatives of the crew had all gathered for a last good-bye. The Cuffe and Wainer clans were there, with Abraham Rodin, a Swedish boy who had apprenticed himself for six years to Paul Cuffe to be "learnt seamanship and other industry." The well-wishers stayed until the *Traveller* sailed out on the two o'clock tide.

A north wind carried the brig south over calm seas past Block Island, Long Island, and the Jersey shore. She rounded Cape May into Delaware Bay and arrived after nine days in Philadelphia. Cuffe sold a cargo of barley for a dollar a bushel. With his profits he purchased more general merchandise until he had a holdful of cargo worth about $4,000, which he hoped would pay for the Sierra Leone voyage.

The Quakers of the Arch Street Meeting, having learned of Cuffe's arrival in Philadelphia, invited him to meet with them. After "a feeling conference, they expressed satisfaction" with Cuffe's plans for Sierra Leone and asked him to call on John James and Alexander Wilson, who had contacted the African Institution for him.

John James said that, as long as Cuffe was finally going to Sierra Leone, he might as well carry a load of corn that James had long held and sell it for him in Portugal or Cadiz. Cuffe explained patiently to the Quaker merchant that "that was not his business. It was not for the profit of grain sales that he had undertaken this voyage." So John James gave up trying to get his corn shipped and told Cuffe he now understood that the *Traveller* was not on a money-making trip.

James even offered to help outfit the *Traveller* without charge. But Cuffe declined, saying he would prefer "if my friends, rather than to burden them, would let me go" without their assistance. Then James heard that good money could be made in Sierra Leone. So he approached Cuffe again with another proposition. He wanted to invest in the voyage. Cuffe said James could have a half share if Alexander Wilson also had a half. James agreed. Then he wrote to London, behind Cuffe's back, complaining to the African Institution about Alexander's being involved.

Cuffe was upset. He needed the goodwill of the African Institution. They, however, retained their confidence in him. Finally he was able, after a month in port, to forget the intrigues of Philadelphia and prepare to sail. The only reminders of Philadelphia he had on board were two passengers for Sierra Leone, Mrs. Catherine Cook and Captain Richardatt.

On January 2, 1811, Paul Cuffe started the new year with new hope by weighing anchor and setting sail for a new land. He was eastward bound at last toward his dream of equality. Blown by a following wind, the *Traveller* moved under easy sail past Bermuda. The waves rolled calmly by for a quiet, uneventful month.

Then on January 30 a high wind rose. Cuffe ordered the canvas shortened. With all the topsails furled, the *Traveller's* tall masts looked as bare as fishbones. By night it had turned stormy. The wind rose to gale force, howling through the rigging "like a legion of devils," raging and shrieking. The seas were blown mountain high. Huge swells swept the ship and soaked the crew.

All hands worked feverishly to take in sail before the canvas was blown to pieces. The sea heaved. The crew hauled on the lines, fighting the fierce wind. Trapped in the teeth of the storm, every timber creaked as the ship was shaken with growling fury. Suddenly a powerful blow laid her over. The churning sea surged over the ship, sweeping John Marsters down the slanting deck. He hooked an elbow around the standing rigging, hung on, and was saved.

The ship rode out the storm safely. When Captain Cuffe saw that all was safe and well, he called the crew together to thank the Lord for their deliverance. The sun rose over the bow, lighting their silent Quaker prayer.

Midway in a life spent fleeing and fighting the horrors of the slave trade, Paul Cuffe found himself storm-stopped in midpassage in the middle of the Atlantic Ocean, halfway between the West Indies and Africa. The storm had struck the *Traveller* in the center of the dread Middle Passage of the slave ships from Africa to the Indies. Paul prayed that this was not an omen.

Was his pride in his own accomplishments so great that he was blind to the possible peril of his plans for his people? Was he taking them forward on a voyage to equality or backward to a slavelike life on a slave-trading continent? Could he teach the Africans how to profit from the produce of the land and sea trade so that they would not have to profit from the trade of their own people? Would they learn or would they revert to their old ways when he sailed away?

If John Marsters' near-death was a warning, then he would accept it as such and survey Sierra Leone with a clear eye. He would not be so blinded by hope that his eyes would not notice any sure signs of certain failure for his project. He would make absolutely certain that his dream was realizable before he arranged for anyone to leave his American home for an African dream.

But the storm proved to be just a storm, and fair winds blew them quickly on toward Sierra Leone. With clear weather and smooth seas, Cuffe spent his time reading Thomas Clarkson's History of the Rise, Progress and Accomplishment of the Abolition of the African Slave Trade by the British Parliament. It hung "very heavy over my head and battered my mind in the sin of his proceedings."

Pushed by pleasant breezes, the Traveller sailed past the Cape Verde Islands. In these fairly frequented waters Cuffe sighted three ships in one day, "standing on our course: the British frigate Amherst, a British convict ship, and a Portuguese ship, Bonsupo, bound to Rajerara."

The gentle breezes held for a month's smooth sailing. Then on February 21 the first fine dust of African soil sifted down through their rigging. Land was only a week away. Now the sun was very hot, and the sea very calm. The sails barely drew, and the men spent their time chasing the small squares of shade that shifted with the sun. The Traveller edged slowly across the burning sea.

The men looked forward to the evening when the scorching sun set, and they brought their hammocks up to sleep on deck. At dawn a shaft of brightness shot up from the horizon. The sky turned pink. The huge red globe of the sun rose quickly and climbed steadily upward in the pearly sky.

On February 25 Captain Cuffe sounded and struck bottom at sixty-five fathoms. The African bottom was black sand mixed with fine sand and coarse gravel. In the torrid heat the crew fished, half hypnotized by the sparkling sea. They caught one dolphin and many sucker fish. That evening they feasted on fish for the first time since they had sailed out of American waters.

Three days later, at noon on the twenty-eighth of February, they spied the steep green mountains of Sierra Leone about thirty-eight miles away. As they approached the northward jutting Sierra Leone Peninsula, they could see the 1,700-foot high Sugar Loaf Mountain. Wooded and wild, it dropped sheer to the dark-edged sea. Majestically dominating the flat featureless West African shore, it seemed appropriately named Sierra Leone, the "Mountain of the Lion," by its Portuguese discoverers.

As the sun rose on the morning of March 1, the *Traveller* sailed into the nutcrackerlike jaws of the mouth of the Sierra Leone River. The river was really the estuary of the Rokel River. The estuary formed a deep inlet that cut into the African coast to create the north shore of the Sierra Leone Peninsula.

Freetown lay nestled against the tree-covered coastal mountains of the peninsula with the inlet at her feet. The river-inlet made a safe, spacious harbor for the town. The *Traveller* entered the Freetown harbor at 8:30 A.M. And Captain Cuffe dropped anchor after fifty-eight days at sea.

8

Freetown

Captain Cuffe gazed around him at the beautiful green-fringed Freetown harbor. It was deep and commodious enough to accommodate many ocean-going vessels. In time Freetown could become a busy, prosperous port. Seeing a small schooner moored nearby, Cuffe guessed that Freetown had already started some coastal trading. Two other trading ships lay anchored offshore. But they had been brought in for illegal slave trading by the English frigate alongside them. On the shore lay two "hulks that had been condemned in the slave trade."

Cuffe waited in the harbor for the governor's permission to land. Governor Columbine was away on the large forested Bance Island at the mouth of the Sierra Leone River. As an ex-naval captain, Columbine was as concerned as his predecessor Governor Thompson had been about the indefensibility of Freetown from outside attack. There was a century-old fort on the island that had long been abandoned by the British and left for the slave traders' use. Columbine wanted to make it into a workable fort again.

The next day Governor Columbine came on board the *Traveller* to welcome Captain Cuffe officially to the British

Crown Colony. He had been informed of Cuffe's voyage by the British Quakers of the powerful African Institution, who had written enthusiastically about his plans. The governor sympathized with some of them, but he lacked the power to grant Cuffe permission to bring black American colonists to the colony. And he definitely did not want any American goods brought into Sierra Leone to compete with British trade.

The Crown was supposed to have a trade monopoly with Freetown, but more supplies entered Sierra Leone from America than from the United Kingdom. Columbine was determined that under his governorship this unauthorized trade would cease. So he gave Captain Cuffe and his crew permission to land, but not to sell their cargo.

Cuffe explained that he carried only enough general merchandise to cover his expenses. The governor then grudgingly granted him permission to sell the perishable portion of his cargo. He sampled Cuffe's American bread and beef, and bought some beef and navy bread for himself. Then he invited Captain Cuffe to dine with him in two days, on the fourth.

After the governor left, Cuffe and his crew visited Freetown. Having been led to expect a primitive shambles, they were pleasantly surprised to find a settled, bustling, colorful town. Planned like a grid, nine streets ran in parallel lines from the harbor to the mountains. Crossing these were three longer main thoroughfares called Water, Oxford, and Westmoreland streets.

The intersecting streets formed rectangular blocks, which were divided into 48-by-76-foot lots. The blocks contained schools, churches, courts, commercial buildings, the government structures started by former Governor Thompson, the stone houses of the prosperous, and the more numerous wooden frame houses built by the Nova Scotians to resemble those left behind back in New England.

The houses were small but carefully built on stone foundations two or three feet off the ground and partitioned into separate rooms. The floors were wood, and the roofs were thatched or shingled, depending on the wealth of the owner. Because the houses were wooden, the food was cooked in the backyard or in a separate cookhouse.

The women not only cooked ouside, they also spent a lot of time visiting outside on their way to market or church. In their bright twisted head scarves and sky-blue bonnets, they added color to the Freetown scene as they jingled through town in their rings and beads of gold, coral, and cut glass. The men visited the numerous public houses and grog shops for the popular local palm wine.

Captain Cuffe advised his men to avoid both the grog shops and the Freetown belles and live on board ship. He kept them busy for two days unloading cargo. Then, after all the permitted cargo had been landed, he left to dine with the governor. Cuffe sat at the governor's table and listened to his complaints about Sierra Leone.

Governor Columbine was an embittered man. London had sent him to replace Thompson as the second governor of the crown colony. He had been given strict instructions to "study, observe, and change such aspects of his predecessor's administration as he saw fit." Columbine concentrated on governmental reform. He wrote London that he could end Freetown's inflation with less government spending and more independent work from the population to increase agricultural production.

He instituted a system of careful accounting of existing stores and current expenditure. But he couldn't get his department head to use his new system and write the weekly reports he needed on government works, the number of workmen employed by each department, their work, and their daily wage.

He had been even more frustrated in his attempts to

71

encourage agriculture. The Liberated Africans, brought in from the slave ships, had continued the process begun by Thompson of moving into the rural areas around Freetown. But their settlements had neither official approval nor recognition, and so were independent of his control.

"As for the Nova Scotians," he complained to Cuffe, "they won't farm because they are all skilled craftsmen or traders. And they won't pay taxes. Yet they demand that the government provide public-work projects to keep their craftsmen employed. They ignore the government and listen only to their dissenting preachers. They are in fact a completely ungovernable, unruly people."

Cuffe replied that of course he was just a visitor, but Freetown appeared to him to be thriving. And the Nova Scotian settlers seemed quite capable of managing their own affairs. When faced with a lack of sufficiently fertile soil and no knowledge of tropical agriculture, they had proved resilient and adaptable in turning to trade. There seemed to be a very lively trade already established with the local population in the interior of the country and along the coast.

Columbine shrugged off Cuffe's observations, saying that trade was impossible with the native tribes, because they were untrustworthy and dangerous. Besides, he was too ill to cope with the situation any longer. The terrible unhealthy climate of Sierra Leone had already killed his wife and daughter, and he was going to leave in May on his own authority if London continued to ignore his request for a replacement.

Cuffe said he was sorry that Sierra Leone had proved such a disaster for the governor and for London, but he was still interested in making an extensive visit of the settlement. Columbine said he didn't advise it, but if Cuffe wished to chance it, he had official permission to travel wherever he wished.

Cuffe rented a house in Freetown from Peter Francis

for £4 per month. Peter Francis was one of the most skilled of the Nova Scotians, an excellent carpenter, who built good, sturdy houses which he rented out, at a handsome profit, to the colony's white officials. Governor Columbine cautioned Cuffe "to be careful to whom he paid the rent, as it was likely that others than the owners would call for the rent."

But Cuffe found the Nova Scotians to be honest and hospitable. Besides, he needed a place on shore to store and sell his cargo and a more convenient home base to travel from than the *Traveller.* He traveled throughout the colony. He dicovered Sierra Leone to be an inviting land of well-watered, well-wooded hills "with the climate well calculated for the cultivation of West-India and other tropical productions."

The settlers mainly cultivated their own gardens, growing cassava and other vegetables for their personal use. Few export crops were grown, though coffee and cotton plants were native to the region and could be successfully raised. The peninsula soil was only moderately fertile. But Sherbro Islands and Mendiland in the southwest were fertile, and Freetown imported food from there to supplement the town's diet.

Freetown also imported dye-yielding camwood and ivory from the interior, where elephants still roamed. Cuffe bartered 2,352 pounds of ivory for the six bales of cloth that he had not been allowed to sell in Freetown. He also bought camwood and firewood for his return cargo. The forests of Sierra Leone contained many varieties of valuable timber trees that Cuffe felt would be another important export for Freetown to add to the camwood and ivory already being exported.

Trade, Cuffe realized, was perhaps the firmest economic foundation for Freetown. Although agriculture and fishing—especially whaling—could be developed. Sierra Leone's long, deeply indented coastline would facilitate any local coastal trade. And the large rivers, which traversed the country in a generally southwesterly direction, made trade with the interior a simple matter.

When not traveling, Cuffe spent his time getting to know the people of Freetown. Far from being ungovernable, he found them to be an extremely well self-governed people with eight schools, six churches, and five courts. There was even an institution for the relief of the poor and disabled.

The independent Nova Scotians had learned early in their experience to question the government and not to depend overmuch on it. Twice uprooted from their homes, they were welded together in a self-governing group by the bitter experience of slavery and government treachery, which they had had in common.

Their only leaders were the preachers of the dissenting religions whom they had followed in Nova Scotia and continued to follow after their removal to Sierra Leone. Their churches were "vital centers of public opinion and communal action"—the political and social centers of Freetown. There were three main congregations—the Baptists, the Methodists, and the Countess of Huntingdon's Connection.

The Baptists were led by David George. Born a Georgia plantation slave, George had won his freedom fighting with the British in the Revolutionary War. He became a preacher in Nova Scotia with a large devoted congregation, which followed him to Sierra Leone when he decided to accept John Clarkson's offer to emigrate in 1791. George liked Clarkson and acted as his second in command on the voyage to Africa. His continued loyalty to Clarkson encouraged his faithful followers to support the government during the Nova Scotian rebellions.

The Baptists remained alone in their support. The Methodist and Huntingdonian Churches led the settlers' opposition to the government. The Huntingdonian Church had been formed during the eighteenth century, when the Countess of Huntingdon led a group of Anglicans in splitting away from the Established Church. Her movement immediately spread to the American colonies and was introduced to Nova Scotia by a free black after the Revolutionary War. The Nova Scotian leaders of the Huntingdonians died after the 1800 settler rebellion in Sierra Leone. The leadership passed to a Maroon, John Ellis, who recruited many of the newly freed slaves into the group.

The largest and most powerful religious and political group in Sierra Leone was the Methodists, who built a four-hundred-seat church in Freetown in 1798. The Methodists had been led from Nova Scotia by old, blind, and lame "Daddy Moses" Wilkinson and his assistant preacher, Luke Jordan, both of whom had escaped from Virginia plantations to Nova Scotia. "Daddy Moses" and Jordan were persistent critics of the government. During the quitrent dispute, they threatened to expel any member of their congregation who paid the government tax.

The Methodist Church was such an effective government critic that many British governors tried to close it down and force the members into the Anglican Church. But none had been able to silence "Daddy Moses" when he "outstretched his voice to terror and frightfulness." Cuffe attended the Methodist Church while in Sierra Leone, and he was impressed by how central the people's religion was to their experience. "Christianity was for them dynamic and personal. The personal experience of the individual and his sharing in fellowship with others— the sense of being the people of God—was a matter of profound importance."

9

Native Tribes

After Governor Columbine's direful warning about the treacherous, dangerous natives, Paul Cuffe was surprised to discover that the interest the neighboring chiefs took in the new settlement was friendly rather than warring. Indeed, two weeks after Captain Cuffe's arrival, King Tom, the chief of the Koya Temne tribe, paid a royal visit to the *Traveller*. King Tom ruled the whole Sierra Leone peninsula, except for the land sold to the colony in 1787 plus the land lost in 1801, when he and the rebelling Nova Scotians had been defeated and King Tom had been forced to cede all his "lands west of Freetown as far as the sea."

King Tom's Temnes were a West Atlantic people who, since the discovery of agriculture, had quietly farmed their steep forest valleys untouched by the ancient empires to the north. When golden Ghana fell to the Mande-speaking Susu Tribe and the new kingdom of Mali rose, the new empire simply took over Ghana's role in developing and controlling the trade between the agricultural and gold-bearing lands of the Negroes and the tribes who controlled the caravan routes across the Sahara.

The Mandingo traders of Mali were famous for their skill and enterprise. They expanded the boundaries of their empire. Mande-speaking traders even penetrated, for the first time, into the deep forests and valleys of Sierra Leone to trade with the coastal tribes for sea salt. The Susu pressed southward to settle close by the coast to the north of Sierra Leone.

In the sixteenth century a group of conquering Mende soldiers, called the Mane, had come from the east, leaving in their wake new societies of mixed Mane and local tribes. The Temne, who had not developed political institutions beyond the village level, took Mane chiefs but kept their local West Atlantic agricultural culture.

The Mane chiefs protected their Temne people militarily. They controlled and distributed the tribal land, made sure that it was properly farmed, and that every tribal member had his proper place and was provided for. The chiefs entertained strangers and judged disputes. The chief's deputy was the speaker, or "mouthpiece." He transmitted the chief's orders and acted as a public-opinion sounding board for the chief. Sudordinate to the speaker were the subchiefs, and under them were the town chiefs and village headmen.

The chief was supposed to consult his council over any measure affecting the chiefdom as a whole. His council was composed of the tribe's elders, to whom the chief was responsible for his actions. But the chief rarely held court with his full council. He relied for his news on the courtiers who took care of him and were known as the chief's "gossipers" and the chief's "eyes and ears."

When the chief left his own compound, he was always accompanied by his courtiers, including his food taster, the "mori"-man who assisted in public sacrifices, and the "Bearer of the Chief's Life," who safeguarded his chief's life and health from witchcraft. The chief wore the leopard-teeth sign of royal rank and was carried in a hammock followed by women singers and male drummers extolling his praises.

The chief displayed all his wealth as proof of his prestige and power to buy the loyalty of others. His people had no need of money. The tribal land belonged to the whole tribe and was administrated by the chief as head of the tribe. The people lived on what they grew and exchanged goods with their neighbors. They knew nothing of private property or private enterprise. They saw no reason to work beyond the mere point of providing for themselves and their families. They were content with their gardens and houses made of stakes stuck in the ground, hardened with mud and covered with thatch.

The houses of the chief and his court were made of hardened clay and brick covered with chalk or white clay. Inside they were whitewashed and the chief's compound was richly furnished with presents from the tribe. In addition to gifts, the chief was entitled to a small portion of every farmer's produce as well as any leopard killed in the chiefdom. He could also claim a small "dash" from anyone tapping palm wine and the fees and fines from court cases. The chiefdom supplied him with labor for his farms and to keep his compound and roads repaired.

All this was sufficient to uphold the chief's dignity until the Portuguese adapted the lateen sail, which enabled them to sail close enough to the wind to explore the windward coast of Africa. With European ships arriving in increasing numbers, Sierra Leone was suddenly transformed from the inaccessible back door of North Africa to the very accessible front door to European trade.

The Mane chiefs had been good traders in the trading empire of Mali, and they proved equally adept at European trade. They allowed no invasion of their territory. All trading was done in coastal trading castles rented by the Europeans from the chiefs. An English sea captain wrote in 1553: "These people are very clever in their bargaining. They use their own weights and measures, and they are very careful how they use them. Anyone who wants to deal with them must do so decently, for they will not trade if they are badly treated."

After Columbus discovered America, Europeans were no longer satisfied with the gold and ivory of West Africa. They wanted slaves for their mines and plantations in the New World. To keep their middleman monopoly, the coastal chiefs had to become slave traders. The slaves, of course, were not taken from their own people but from the interior tribes. The chiefs remained independent, and the secluded anchorages of Sierra Leone's coastal inlets and islands encouraged trade with independently owned ships that owed no allegiance to any of the great national trading companies of Europe.

But as the demand for slaves grew, so did the dependence of the coastal chiefs upon the degrading slave trade. To supply the increased demand they had to make wars to obtain captives. And to make the wars, they needed the guns supplied only by the slavers. The slave trade turned into a vicious circle that broke down tribal social structures, security, and self-respect.

By 1796 sea merchants were writing that the coastal Africans of Sierra Leone "are in general shrewd and artful, sometimes malevolent and perfidious. Their long connection with European slave traders has tutored them in the arts of deceit, so that false weights and measures, damaged goods, and all the various cheats which the ingenuity of the more enlightened European has strained itself to invent, are now detected almost as soon as they are attempted."

Paul Cuffe felt tremendously encouraged by King Tom's visit. Governor Columbine had cast so pessimistic a pall over Sierra Leone's future that Cuffe had wondered if his dream of freeing West Africa from its dependence on the slave trade was possible. He had hoped that if the traffic in slaves could be stopped, slavery would begin to disappear in America. He knew that despite the British naval patrols, slaves were still being exported from West Africa in considerable numbers. But he thought that if a new thriving triangular trade could be established among Africa, the United States, and Europe, based on native African products, it could displace the slave trade.

Now with King Tom making the first encouraging move, Cuffe might be able to convince the king and the other Sierra Leone chiefs that there were other less destructive and equally profitable trades to be developed instead of the slave trade. So he feasted the grave old king and his retinue of thirteen and presented him with a book of essays on war and a history of slavery by the Quaker Elizabeth Webb. As he talked with the king, Cuffe supplemented the conversation with a pamphlet and "a letter of advice from myself such as appeared to me to be good to hand to the King for the use and encouragement of the nations of Africa."

The next day King George of the Bulloms sent his messenger to the *Traveller,* with three chickens and an invitation to dinner. The Bulloms were one of the earliest and most powerful tribes in Sierra Leone. But like the Temnes, they too had been conquered by the invading Mane soldiers. The Mane created a new Mande-type kingdom of Bullom on the north bank of the Sierra Leone River. The kings were Mane. The native Bulloms were known as Sapes.

A Portuguese report of 1506 describes the Bullom people of Sierra Leone as warlike folk who dealt in gold, which they bought from the inland tribes in exchange for salt. They then traded the gold to the Portuguese for brass rings, large basins, and cotton goods. "And in this country you can buy ivory necklaces that are carved better than anywhere else."

The Mane soldier kings made the Bullom's flat low-lying wooded land into a fortress. Every settlement was strongly stockaded. Paths leading to towns were narrow and overgrown. Roads were made easy to block, and the one gate into town was just wide enough for a man to squeeze through. The houses in the town were built close together like a maze, and the whole town was encircled by three fences. The outer fence was not defended, for it was meant to serve only as a temporary brake on attackers. The inner two fences were guarded by war boys stationed at intervals behind each one.

The soldiers did two days' duty at a time at the fence. They had to cook their own food, because no women were allowed between the war fences. If the war chief convinced the town elders of the necessity for war and they agreed to support an attack, then the principal warriors would take their women along with their swords, spears, and shields. For protection the warriors relied on numerous charms worn all over their bodies.

Spies were sent out first to listen to women's gossip at the water places, in order to discover the weakest point of the war fences. Then the attackers would sneak there with their ladders and vaulting poles for a surprise attack. If the people inside a town learned that an attack was imminent, their besieged chief could decide to resist or sue for peace. If he wanted a truce, he would send his most valued woman with a white cloth, a gun, and some salt, and she would become the wife of the conqueror.

If the war chief decided to fight, then morale would be strengthened by war dancing and sacrifices, and the women and children would be shut up in the women's houses. If the attackers won, the victors danced around the town, then stabbed the bravest defenders as they were led through the fences. The captured women, children, and plunder were brought before the war chief for division among his warriors.

In 1567 the English captain Sir John Hawkins made a slave raid down the Guinea coast. When he reached Sierra Leone, the Mane king asked his help in attacking a town. "This town was built after the use of the country, very warlike and was walled round with mighty trees bound together with great whythes." The besieged had made "false ditches covered with light sticks, leaves and such trumpery, to overthrow our men in and with their envenomed arrows and darts so defended the walls, having made loopes in every place to shoot out at." But Hawkins won by setting the town on fire. Then he sailed with 470 captives to sell as slaves in the West Indies.

All the attacking and defending was fine for testing each warrior's worth, but it did not hold the kingdom together. The cohesive force in the north was the religion of Islam, but Sierra Leone was still mainly pagan. So the controlling force was supplied by Poro. Poro controlled the supernatural power of spirits and medicine. Its leading officers possessed medicines of great strength and communicated with the spirit world, which they impersonated with masks.

Every boy had to leave home and be reborn as a Poro man. The boys stayed together unsheltered out in the bush from November until May. They were instructed in family and social duties and learned drumming and Poro songs. At the end of their initiation, after being swallowed by the Poro spirit, they were placed under the Poro oath.

The oath bound them to whatever plans the society's inner council of senior members had decided upon in secret. Membership extended throughout Sierra Leone. So Poro was the only means by which a uniform system of government and set of customs was possible among Sierra Leone's many warring tribes and scattered communities. All warfare had to stop while Poro was in session. And chiefdoms could combine in Grand Poro to make or stop war.

There was a Poro prohibition on the harvesting of palm fruit and on fishing at certain seasons. Poro regulated trade and fixed prices for commodities and services.

It ensured the maintenance of customary law and behavior and watched the chief to be sure that his actions as ruler conformed with customary practice.

The chief, on his part, was expected to hold the Poro in check and to see that its officials did not take advantage of their mystical power by exploiting the people. Political power was thus balanced between monarchy and Poro. The chiefs and his officials handled the everyday civil management of the country, and Poro dealt with the crises of life and its hidden spiritual forces.

The female equivalent of the Poro was the Bundu Society. Every girl had to enter the Bundu Bush for a course of initiation into the functions of wife, mother, and housekeeper. The Bundu Society held an influential position in tribal life, because women were important in Sierra Leone. Women were good traders. So wives were considered more of an asset than a luxury. An important sign of a chief's status was a large number of wives.

Captain Cuffe crossed the Sierra Leone River to the lowland, or Bullom Shore, opposite Freetown, taking with him his nephew, Henry Wainer, John Morgan, a Maroon from Jamaica, and David Edmonds, a Nova Scotian who ran a thriving shipbuilding business in Freetown. Later he described their reception to friends:

> King George received and treated us very cordially. He appeared to be very friendly. He could speak but very little English himself, but had a young man with him who had received his education in England, and appeared to be a man of very good information. This tribe seem to acknowledge by words the existence of a Diety. So accustomed are they to wars and slavery that I apprehended it would be a difficult task to convince them of the impropriety of these pernicious practices.

So Cuffe gave the king a Bible.

10

To Liverpool

In Freetown Paul Cuffe met members of other tribes, not native to Sierra Leone. They had come, like the Mandingo, to trade, or, like the Kru, to find work. The Mandingo were a distinctive people. Even from a distance their height and lighter skin set them apart from the other traders in the Freetown marketplace. Longer-legged, slimmer, often bearded, with aquiline noses and delicate hands and feet, the Mandingo seemed closer in origin to the North African Arabs than to the short-legged, thickset, flat-nosed, and thick-lipped Bantu tribes of Sierra Leone.

But what made the Muslim Mandingo memorable for Paul Cuffe was their religion. "The Mandingo men have the scripture at their tongue, the Old Testament, but they deny the New Testament. They own Mohammed Prophet." The Mandingo or "Mande people" had come from the southern reaches of the great Mali Empire, which once had stretched from the northern desert to the southern forest fringe.

Until the early sixteenth century, Mali was a prosperous, peaceful, well-governed empire with organized communications and trading routes. But it encompassed too many diverse groups, who did not have a natural tradition of belonging together. The Mali Mansas, or kings, were reluctant to use their universal Muslim religion as the binding force to hold all their disparate tribes together. Islam demanded the reading of the Koran and absolute allegiance to its laws first—before family or tribe.

Islam could have been as effective as Poro was to the Mane in Sierra Leone in holding the Mali Empire together. But the Mansas did not forcibly convert to Islam the illiterate pagan people under their control for fear of losing the allegiance of the native gold miners and farmers on whom the Mali Empire was dependent for its wealth.

The Mali court and merchants were Muslim. There were educated and cultured Muslim communities in the cities and towns. But the tribal people of Mali were not converted until the sixteenth century, when the Emperor Askia Mohammed extended his empire to embrace the westward lands and the Muslim religion.

When Askia Mohammed died, Mali collapsed. Trade shifted from the north across the Sahara to the Atlantic Ocean. Power and initiative followed the trade shift. The defenseless Mandingo people were scatttered. So many fell prey to seventeenth-century slavers that in Mexico all slaves were known as Mandingos. Today, the word "Mandingo" is the Mexican name for a devil.

The Mandingos who fled southwest settled among the forest tribes of northern Sierra Leone. They carried with them their passionate love of music. Many Mandingo musical instruments came originally from ancient Egypt, as did their Egyptian oxen with the long, erect horns. The Mandingo shared their skill in metal and leather working with the forest tribes, but they did not wish to mix with them. They preferred to retain their own totem tribal system with a separate identifying plant or animal totem for each tribe or clan.

Paul Cuffe found the Mandingo to be "men of considerable learning. They do not allow spirituous liquors to be made use of in this tribe. They have declined the practice of selling their own tribe, but notwithstanding this, they continue to sell those of other tribes, and thought it hard that the traffic in slaves should be abolished, as they were made poor in consequence thereof."

As the Mandingo were being pushed southwest from their northern homeland, the Kru were crossing Sierra Leone's southern border from their coastal homeland in what is now Liberia. The Kru had been conquered by the same Mane wave that had washed over Sierra Leone in the sixteenth century. But by the time the Mane army had reached the Kru's land, it had become so diluted with non-Mane recruits that the Kru were able to retain more of their own identity than had the tribes native to Sierra Leone.

The Kru still spoke their original Kwa language and worked at their traditional occupations of farming and fishing. They had so great a reputation as skilled boatmen that even the Europeans were impressed. In 1808 Governor Thompson, in an attempt to turn the new crown colony of Sierra Leone into a profit-making enterprise, established a Kru colony in Freetown. He brought the hard-working, honest, seafaring Kru to the only natural harbor in West Africa in the hope of providing Freetown with a fishing industry.

The Kru came and kept on coming because they could scarcely scratch out more than a subsistence living in their own country. They lived apart in Freetown in compounds large enough to house any recently arrived fellow tribesmen. To help each other they elected an absentee tribal headman so that they would not be deprived of tribal benefits while away from home, and would have a spokesman to represent them to the Sierra Leone government.

Paul Cuffe liked the Kru and hired them to help his crew with ship chores. He paid them $3.00 a month and their captain $4.00. Cuffe found all the native tribesmen to be helpful, but the Kru were especially easy to work with. It wasn't the natives who were threatening the prosperity of Freetown and its settlers. It was the whites.

The colony had great possibilities. But the whites were exploiting the settlers and the natives with money-making enterprises that returned enormous profits only to themselves. Cuffe believed that if the colony were freed from this exploitation, Freetown could become a prosperous-enough farming, fishing, and trading community to support many new American settlers. So he helped the settlers draw up a petition for Governor Columbine:

> 1st. That encouragement may be given to all our brethren, who may come from the British colonies or from America, in order to become farmers, or to assist us in the cultivation of our land.
>
> 2d. That encouragement may be given to our foreign brethren who have vessels for the purpose, to establish commerce in Sierra Leone.
>
> 3d. That those who may undertake to establish the whole Fishery in the Colony may be encouraged to persevere in that useful and laudable enterprise.

The whites were furious. Cuffe might ruin all their schemes. He had to be stopped! They tried harassment first. Cuffe found himself so snarled in official red tape that he despaired of ever getting his permitted cargo of bread, meat, and flour sold. The whites thought he would give up and return to America. He almost did.

But Cuffe decided that his dream was too important to abandon so abruptly. He bartered what cargo he could for ivory and hardwood. He started the crew "heeling, hogging, and lead topping" the *Traveller* to ready her for an ocean voyage—not to America but to Great Britain. He would not let himself be defeated by British red tape when he had powerful friends in Britain who could cut through it at the source. His correspondents in the African Institution might also be able to obtain the necessary licenses, permits, and so forth that were needed to make Freetown a prosperous commercial port.

To stop Cuffe the Sierra Leone whites tried sabotage. One official even went to the extreme of writing a poison-pen letter about Cuffe to a leading member of the African Institution in London. The letter warned the African Institution to "be on their guard against any representations that Captain Cuffe might make, as no credit whatever should be attached to anything he might say." The writer added that he "had never known a more mercenary or unprincipled man, except perhaps a slave-trader."

Unaware of the slander, which would follow him for two and a half years, Captain Cuffe sailed for England on May 11, 1811. The voyage was blessed by good omens. The weather remained fair and the sea full of fish. Cuffe noted in his journal that in June a rainbow was sighted "which God placed as a token that the world should not be destroyed with a deluge or overflow of waters again." In July he noted that the sperm whales they saw "appeared to be in very good mood."

Off the coast of Africa the *Traveller* sailed through seaweed and sunsquall and man-of-war jellyfish. Captain Cuffe was following the same warm ocean currents that English slavers had sailed in the heyday of the infamous Great Circuit triangular trade route from Liverpool to West Africa to the West Indies to England. He was traveling back over the first leg of the triangle, over which were carried cheap manufactured goods to West Africa to be exchanged for slaves, which in turn were carried across the dreaded Middle Passage to the West Indies and there traded for sugar, tobacco, and rum, which brought fabulous profits to the Liverpool merchants back home.

Liverpool owed its development and prosperity almost entirely to the slave trade. In the eighteenth century it was said that "almost every man in Liverpool is a merchant." Those who were not were building the ships for the transport of slaves. In 1719 the port of Liverpool had 18,371 tons of registered shipping. By 1792 this rose to 260,382 tons. And it was the Great Circuit trade that commissioned most of the new tonnage.

In one decade from 1783 to 1793 Liverpool slavers made a profit of about £2,360,000 on the shipping of about 303,000 slaves. The enormous cash return from a small capital investment in the slave trade made a new monied merchant class in Britain that not only spent lavishly in glittering displays of wealth but also used its money to buy seats in Parliament and posts of influence. These new rich intended to make their voices heard and their slavery policy an important affair of state.

The few British Quakers who raised horrified voices against the moral iniquities of the slave trade went unheard. The Catholic Church did not prohibit the possession of slaves. Protestant churches, like the Church of England, were so committed to the protection of the rights of property owners that they accepted the notion that slaves were property just like cattle.

Most of the English had never seen a slave, so they accepted the slavers' argument that the slave trade was a vested interest vital to England's prosperity. But the moral campaign of the Quaker abolitionists exposed the horrors of the slave trade and mobilized public and political opinion against it. It was thanks to their efforts that the African slave trade was made illegal as early as 1807. And their friendship and support made it possible, only four years later, for Paul Cuffe to find a friendly welcome in the former slave port of Liverpool.

On June 30, 1811, near the mouth of St. George's Channel off the Scilly Islands of England, a sail was sighted off the weather bow. She was the ship *Fanna*, nine days from Liverpool, bound for Newfoundland. The

Fanna "gave us the unhappy news of an engagement having taken place between one of the United States frigates
and his British Majesty's ship of war off Sandy Hook."

The battle off Sandy Hook was a prelude to the war
of 1812. Ever since Britain had gained control of the seas,
after Nelson defeated Napoleon's navy at Trafalgar,
America's relations with Britain had worsened. The United
States tried to remain neutral and trade with both sides,
but Britain stopped American ships on the high seas, con-
fiscated their cargoes, and "impressed" seamen she
thought—or pretended to think—were British subjects.

The United States lost many seamen through British
impressment. American anger was at the flash point in
1807 when four English seamen jumped ship to escape
the brutal treatment and intolerable conditions aboard
the King's ships. The four signed on the United States
frigate *Chesapeake,* sailing for the Mediterranean.

A few miles off the Virginia Capes, the *Chesapeake*
was hailed by H.M.S. *Leopard* with a demand for the
surrender of the four deserters. The demand was refused,
and the *Leopard* opened fire. Three Americans were killed
and eighteen wounded. The *Leopard* then insolently
boarded the American frigate to seize the men, and the
crippled *Chesapeake* returned home to an enraged
America.

To prevent war, President Thomas Jefferson placed
an embargo on United States ships and ordered all British
warships out of American waters. The embargo was a
failure. So Jefferson replaced it with the Non-Intercourse
Act, which reopened trade with all nations except France
and Britain. But Britain continued to stop American ships
and impress American seamen.

On May 1, 1811, the British frigate *Guerrière* overhauled the American brig *Spitfire* and impressed an
American seaman. The U.S.S. *President,* coming to the
rescue, mistook the British corvette *Little Belt* for the

Guerrière and opened fire off Sandy Hook. The *Little Belt* was disabled, nine of her crewmen were killed, and twenty-three were wounded.

Americans were elated. They saw the *President's* victory as sweet revenge for the *Chesapeake's* defeat. Paul Cuffe did not believe the British would see it that way. He feared trouble, but hoped the conflict off Sandy Hook would not compromise his visit to Britain and cancel his plans for Sierra Leone.

11

England

On July 11 a thick fog settled over the *Traveller*. No breeze stirred her slack sails or ruffled the smooth sea. The muffled sound of a horn drum and a cannon firing warned that land was near. But where? At midnight the wind suddenly breezed forth. The fog parted, and the Skerries Light was sighted. The tiny Skerries Islands guarded the entrance to Liverpool Bay. The *Traveller* tacked toward their light. Then the fog closed in again.

Eastward lay the English shore. Captain Cuffe fired his gun for a pilot to escort the *Traveller* safely into Liverpool Harbor. But none would venture out in the fog. As the crew waited, they celebrated the landfall, after sixty-two days at sea, by killing and feasting on the pig they had brought from Africa. Paul Cuffe did not feel very festive. He wondered what would happen when the fog did lift and what their welcome would be on shore.

The next day, at two in the afternoon, a pilot came on board. Twelve hours later the *Traveller* passed the rocks at the entrance to Liverpool Harbor. At 3 A.M. the customhouse boat came alongside. Finally, at four in the morning, they docked. Their safe uneventful voyage was at an end.

What was to begin was neither safe nor uneventful. As soon as two of Cuffe's crew passed through the dock gate, they were seized and carried away by a press gang.

Press gangs lurked in every port in England to seize seamen for the Royal Navy. The victims had no way of releasing themselves from this involuntary servitude except by mutilation and death. England had lost so many men battling with France and conditions were so bad aboard English warships that impressment was the only way the Royal Navy could complete crews for its ships.

In 1812 the American "war hawks" would demand war with Britain over this question of British impressment of American seamen. But when the press gang came on board the *Traveller,* it was still 1811, and Captain Cuffe could not prevent them from searching his ship for one more "British subject." They found one—he was Aaron Richards, an African who had come with Cuffe as an apprentice to learn navigation. The press gang took him away.

Cuffe followed, in hopes of rescuing the first two of his missing crew—no sensible man could claim *them* to be British subjects. The authorities agreed with Cuffe and were quite willing to return the first two. But the hapless African was another matter. To get Aaron back, Cuffe would need influential help. The Liverpool members of the African Institute were sympathetic but powerless. He would have to look elsewhere for aid.

While Paul Cuffe worked to free Aaron, the people of Liverpool were arranging a celebrity's welcome for the *Traveller.* The ship's arrival had caused a sensation. The English had never before seen a black American sea captain and an all-black crew. So while official Liverpool harassed Cuffe and his men, the people invited them here, there, and everywhere.

The *Times* of London wrote in some surprise that it found Cuffe to be of "an agreeable countenance, and his physiognomy truly interesting; he is both tall and stout, speaks English well, dresses in the Quaker style, in a drab-colored suit, and wears a large flapped white hat."

A Scottish newpaper reported that Cuffe was "said to be very skilled both in trade and navigation, as well as to be of a very pious and moral character." Then, unable to resist a poke at the English, the Scottish paper pointedly added: "It must have been a strange and animating spectacle to see this free and enlightened African entering, as an independent trader, with his black crew, into that port which was so lately the spider's nest of the Slave trade."

The English Quakers and abolitionists were particularly pleased and excited by Cuffe's arrival. One Quaker wrote:

> During the time I have been at Liverpool, Paul Cuffe, a black man, owner and master of a vessel has come into port. He is a member of our Society of Friends and resides in New England. The whole of his crew are black also. This, together with the cleanliness of his vessel, and the excellent order prevailing on board, has excited very general attention. It has, I believe, opened the minds of many in tender feelings toward the poor suffering Africans, who, they see, are men like themselves, capable of becoming, like Paul Cuffe, valuable and useful members both of civil and religious society.

The Quaker abolitionists in Liverpool saw Paul Cuffe as the perfect promoter of their plans for freeing Africa from the evils of the slave trade and making it a democratic Christian continent. Impressed with the depth of Cuffe's mind, his quick grasp of things, and his simplicity of manner, they wrote glowing reports to their colleagues in London: "The present opportunity for promoting the civilization of Africa, through the means of Paul Cuffe, should not be lost. He seems like a man made on purpose for the business. He has great experience as well as integrity."

When England's leading abolitionists expressed an interest in meeting Paul Cuffe, the African Institution decided he should travel at once to London for a specially convened meeting with their members. Cuffe agreed to leave Liverpool immediately. He saw the London meeting as the best way of freeing Aaron and obtaining the necessary backing for his Sierra Leone plans.

The London stagecoach left Liverpool at ten in the evening. It was a long but pleasant summer journey through the beautifully tended, gardenlike countryside around Stratford and Oxford. The horses were changed every ten to fifteen miles. So the coach moved at a steady, tireless pace that quickly shortened the 208 miles to London. The constantly changing scenery chased away boredom, and the many stops for food and drink, at public houses along the way, gave ample opportunity for stretching travel-weary legs.

Cuffe, who was a careful investor and spender of money, learned on the journey about the strange English custom of tipping. He was expected, he discovered, to give threepence to the servants in each public house and sixpence to the coach drivers and watchmen when they changed at fifty-mile intervals. The tipping made his expenses mount up to twenty-three shillings for the trip plus the £4 17s for his fare.

The three-day trip ended at 6 A.M. Cuffe found a London inn and had breakfast. At ten he met William Allen, his first and most constant supporter in Britain. William Allen was a wealthy scientist devoted to helping those unable to help themselves. He fed the poor, reformed the schools, opposed capital punishment, and was a founder of the African Institution. It was Allen who had encouraged Cuffe to go to Sierra Leone and seek backing from the African Institution.

William Allen had been trying to liberate Aaron without success. He suggested that Cuffe ask Britain's most famous philanthropist, William Wilberforce, for help. Wilberforce, Thomas Clarkson, and Granville Sharp had been the trio most responsible for the abolition of the English slave trade. Since Wilberforce had asked to meet Cuffe, Cuffe could certainly feel free to ask his help.

The next day Cuffe spoke to Wilberforce about Aaron. The philanthropist called at once for pen, ink, and paper and wrote to the Board of Admiralty, then sent his man without delay to the notary. When no news came of Aaron's release, Cuffe went to the second member of the famous trio, Thomas Clarkson. Clarkson had written the definitive book on the slave trade that Cuffe had read with great interest and emotion on the voyage to Sierra Leone.

Thomas Clarkson introduced Cuffe to his younger brother, John, who had brought the first Nova Scotian settlers to Sierra Leone. Then Clarkson promised to go to the First Lord of the Admiralty, where he found the order had already gone out for Aaron's discharge. So Clarkson had friends look after Aaron until he was back aboard the *Traveller*.

With Aaron safe, Cuffe could concentrate on Sierra Leone. He wished to be fully prepared for his presentation before the African Institution. The institution members were interrupting their summer vacations to reconvene hastily in London to meet Cuffe. His Royal Highness the Duke of Gloucester dashed into London from his country retreat to preside over this conference with his "dark-coloured but civilized ally." Cuffe presented the Duke with an African robe, a letter box, and a dagger to impress him with the skills and intelligence most Africans possessed.

Then Cuffe discussed the best way of encouraging the improvement of the Sierra Leone colony. He pleaded that the colonists needed help and encouragement. He stressed the necessity of establishing commerce in Africa, and "the necessity of keeping open a communication between America, Africa and England in order to assist Africa in its civilization." This communication and trade with Africa should continue even if America and England went to war. African trade could be considered "as a neutral path. And the French government, too, may rejoin the neutral path."

To keep trade and "a channel of intercourse open between America and Sierra Leone," Cuffe proposed to build a ship and "a house in Sierra Leone in order that if the way should open for a family to come to Sierra Leone, encouragement might be given of accommodation, and by their gently getting along, might the better and with more ease encourage still other people to go to that country."

The members of the African Institution were delighted with their "articulate black American associate." He made "very sensible and satisfactory answers" to their questions. "And his simplicity and strong natural good sense made a great impression upon all parties." They "expressed great satisfaction in the information" Cuffe had given them.

Then they voted to forward immediately a petition to the Privy Council to obtain a license for the *Traveller* to go to Africa. After cutting through the red tape in England, they arranged for the petty officials in Sierra Leone to give Cuffe no more trouble. They wrote to the Freetown authorities concerning Cuffe and their endorsement of his trading mission. The Duke was so impressed with Cuffe that "after the Captain had withdrawn, a vote of thanks was passed to him, and a committee appointed to see what use might be made of him."

Cuffe was elated with the success of his London visit. Thanks to the intervention of the African Institution, he would soon receive official permission from the British government to develop his African dream. While Cuffe waited for the arrival of his African trading license, his friends took him sightseeing.

He was given the usual tour of the city—the Houses of Parliament, the Tower of London, London Bridge, Hyde Park Zoo, and the national mint. His interest was chiefly aroused by the mint. He was fascinated by the huge steam engines stamping out sixty to seventy guineas in a minute.

It was the port of London he most wanted to see, especially the shipping and accommodations of the London and West India docks. That was a sight that really aroused his enthusiasm. To see a broad river, a quarter mile wide, full of ships as far as the eye could see, was not a sight you could see in New Bedford, where the whole town turned out whenever each ship arrived.

He also found his visit to Lancaster's London School interesting. It was, he said, "the greatest gratification that I met with." Here a whole new system of inexpensive education was being tried out. Only one teacher was needed for one thousand students, because the students themselves were doing the teaching, the less advanced learning from the more advanced. It meant that many children could now go to school who had not been able to afford to before.

Besides sightseeing, Cuffe was busy buying tea and sundry merchandise for cargo. When he went to settle his cargo account, he was asked "whether I should have any more business with them. I answered: as to that, I was uncertain. My business was small, and as to using flattery to deceive him, that was not my way of doing business. Lubbuck then took my account and allowed 2½ per cent discount. I find honesty," reflected Cuffe, "to be the best policy."

Cuffe decided to buy more cargo merchandise from the Manchester cotton mills. He bought an inside seat in the Manchester stagecoach for four guineas. There were four people sitting inside and fourteen riding outside in the half-price seats. The coach left at two in the afternoon. He said good-bye to his London friends, who gave him a box of eighty books as a farewell present.

It rained all night. After an eight o'clock breakfast, they rode through "low land fogs and cool chilly vapor risings of the low land." Before they dined again at 6 P.M., the coach passed through the town of Tedbury where a woman had lived "4 years without eating, 3½ years without drinking, 2 years and 10 months without sleeping." Or so local gossip claimed.

Cuffe arrived in Manchester at eight in the evening. The next day he visited the cotton mills, and was impressed with their modern technology:

> They light the darkest room with gas extracted from sea coal. This light far exceeds the candlelight. It is more like daylight. The air issues out of a small tube. And by the blaze of a candle being put to it, it blazes and burns until the gas is stopped. This is done by turning the stop that reaches through the pipe.

Cuffe stayed only two days in Manchester, then took the 6 A.M. stage for the thirty-six-mile, four-hour trip to Liverpool. Arriving at 10 A.M., he "found the people all well, as well on board the vessel as in the city." He was particularly delighted to see Aaron Richards safe back on the *Traveller* after his terrifying abduction.

With all seemingly well and shipshape, Cuffe spent the night with the Rathbones. The elder Rathbone and his two sons were public-spirited Quakers who had actively opposed the slave trade and fought for municipal reform. They were fascinated with Cuffe and made their home his home, helping him whenever and however they could. When the Rathbone sons became convinced that Cuffe was an "instrument of God sent to England to lead the cause of African emancipation," Cuffe felt he had to warn them "that the flesh was imperfect, and forewarned is to be forearmed, and they were not to put too great confidence in me as I was but flesh and blood."

Captain Cuffe spent the September days before his departure preparing his ship and cargo. While the *Traveller* was hauled out on the bank to "grime," Cuffe visited friends and places he had not been to before, such as the pottery factory and the blind school. He found the blind students to be a great inspiration, who accomplished much despite their handicap.

All seemed ready for departure, but at the last minute John Marsters (who had so nearly been washed overboard on the way to Sierra Leone) decided he did not wish to return to Africa. Then the *Traveller* had to wait two days for a late delivery of the cotton goods Cuffe had ordered in Manchester. When the ship was once more ready to clear port, its five passengers were not. Four passengers were Methodist missionary teachers; the fifth, an African boy named Bango Burso, was returning home to the coast of Burso.

At last on September 20, 1811, the sails were set, the anchor was up, and the *Traveller* was under weigh. A small breeze carried the ship slowly away from the wharf, which was crowded with Cuffe's friends waving a last good-bye. They had become very fond of Cuffe during his all-too-brief stay. William Allen said sadly, "We had an affecting parting, as it is not very probable we shall see him any more."

12

The Return

The return to Sierra Leone, Cuffe discovered, was much more difficult than the "going o'er" to England. It rained for forty days and forty nights. Constant squalls "entangled the sails," sickened the passengers, and frayed the tempers of the crew. Zachariah White, who had been suspected of drinking to excess in Liverpool, picked a fight with Cuffe's nephew and first mate, John Wainer. Cuffe separated them and later found many empty bottles among the port stored in the hold. "It seems to me," Cuffe wrote in his journal, "there had been great thirst while in the hold."

The *Traveller* appeared to be alone in the deep. A thick curtain of rain and mountainous seas hid any other vessels from view. The only thing sighted was an iron-bound, barnacled hogshead thrown up by the heaving sea. No one wanted to think about the ship that it had been separated from for so long. Cuffe noted in his journal that "a heavy jumbled sea with an enveloping gale has been the general cause of the trial of our patience. Since leaving Liverpool our passengers hath pretty well buried their appetites."

Finally, on the last day of October, the weather cleared. They were nearing the African coast, and the weather was African—calm and hot. Fierce, ravenous sharks appeared. A ten-foot-long black porpoise was harpooned. When a piece of the porpoise was hung over the stern, a shark tried to take it away. Cuffe shot the shark. "After a small fling, it sank immediately out of sight."

On November 12, 1811, after fifty-three days at sea, land was sighted off the starboard bow. Cape Sierra Leone was only two leagues away, but the tide was ebbing and the wind was offshore, so Cuffe anchored. At 1 P.M. the tide changed, and the *Traveller* sailed with it into Freetown Harbor. Three hours later the ship was boarded by Cuffe's nephew, Thomas Wainer, who had stayed behind to supervise Cuffe's Sierra Leone ventures.

Wainer was accompanied by David Edmonds, a second-generation Nova Scotian shipbuilder who had come to welcome Cuffe's English passengers to Freetown. The Nova Scotian Methodists had waited seven years for this arrival. Every year since 1804, they had asked their parent church in London to send them a religious leader and schoolmasters. Now, at long last, Cuffe had brought them the Reverend George Warren and his three teaching associates to direct Methodist activities in Freetown.

Their own preacher, old Daddy Moses Wilkinson, and his helper Luke Jordan, had led them across the Atlantic to Sierra Leone. But the congregation was larger now. It filled the four-hundred-seat Methodist chapel for four Sunday services and daily evening prayer meetings. The daily life of the Nova Scotian Methodists centered on their church. It was the hub of their social and political activities. But it was too great a burden for their two preachers to carry alone. They needed help.

When England first undertook to govern Sierra Leone, the colonial governor was ordered to close the Methodist chapel and force its congregation to worship in Freetown's Anglican church. The Nova Scotians flatly refused to enter the Church of England, and eventually their chapel was opened. But all religious services were forbidden after 8 P.M. and before 5 A.M. "either in private houses or public places."

The governors of Sierra Leone believed that all His Majesty's colonial subjects ought to belong to the established Church of England. If the Methodists could not be forced into joining, perhaps they could be persuaded. So the government asked the Church Missionary Society to send an Anglican missionary to Sierra Leone.

The missionary arrived in 1804. He regularly preached in the Anglican church, collected fees as the parish clerk, served as chaplain to the white community, and taught in the government-sponsored school. His teaching made the school enrollment grow from 20 to over 150 pupils. He even opened evening classes for Maroon adults. The Methodists could only counter his success with a school and missionary of their own. For seven years they had asked for one, and now he had finally arrived. The Nova Scotians were overjoyed. The new governor was not.

The new governor was Colonel Charles William Maxwell. Maxwell had been the military commandant at Senegal when he was appointed to the governorship of Sierra Leone on July 1, 1811. Maxwell replaced Captain Columbine who, ill and discouraged, had left without leave in May just as he had warned he would. But Columbine never reached England. He died of fever in mid-passage and was buried at sea in June.

Maxwell was Sierra Leone's sixteenth governor in nineteen years. Such frequent changes in command caused comment in Britain. It was said that Sierra Leone always had two governors, one just arrived in Africa and the other just arrived in England. Some of the governors died of fever, but many quit in frustration over Britain's colonial policy.

After Britain abolished the slave trade in 1807, its African foreign policy changed from promotion of trade to suppression of the slave trade. This negative policy obviously wasn't working. Slaves were still being exported from the west coast of Africa in considerable numbers, despite all the Royal Navy patrols.

Now British abolitionists joined with the new Protestant missionary societies to urge a change in policy. They said the slave trade could be stopped if stable conditions were substituted, in which peaceful trade and orderly development could take place. They summed up their policy in three words: Christianity, commerce, and colonization. They wanted to convert the West Africans to Christianity, develop a substitute trade for the slave trade to compensate British slavers for their losses, and establish pioneer West African communities to demonstrate good methods of agriculture, industry, and government.

The British government applauded the plan but refused to finance it. Members of Parliament were aware that the economy-minded taxpayers who elected them would not support any increased activity in West Africa. The governors of the African crown colonies were told to support the policies of the abolitionists and missionaries, but they were given no money to do so.

The British navy continued to bring all arrested slavers to trial in the special courts set up for that purpose in Freetown. After punishing the guilty slavers and freeing their cargo of slaves, the government felt its duty had been done. The liberated captives were free to go wherever they wished, and if the homelands from which they had been snatched were hundreds of miles away, in distant parts of Africa, that was not the government's fault. Most of the Liberated Africans stayed on in Sierra Leone, because they had no way to get home or did not know where it lay exactly or feared recapture if they tried to find it.

By 1811, when Maxwell became governor, over twelve

hundred Liberated Africans had been released in Sierra Leone. The missionaries reported that the poor health and near starvation of the recent captives resulted in many deaths and increased the danger to other colonists. But with the Crown insisting that costs be held to a minimum, Governor Maxwell could not feed them all.

Nor could he govern them effectively. Many settled outside Freetown and formed communities that lay beyond his control. If he could not govern them, then he could not help them. They defied all his attempts to make Sierra Leone an efficient administrative entity.

The rebelliously independent Nova Scotians were worse. They were never satisfied. They complained constantly about the Liberated Africans stealing their property and were every bit as ungovernable as the newcomers. Now they had brought in a Methodist minister from Britain to lead them and Methodist schoolmasters to teach their children more free thinking.

Maxwell knew he would have to deal with them immediately—and the troublemaking black captain they sailed with. The British government demanded promotion of trade. The African Institution demanded cooperation with this man Cuffe. As a mercantilist, Maxwell too wanted to promote trade, but not with a Yankee trader who would funnel all the profits to America.

Two hours after anchoring, Captain Cuffe and his four passengers went on shore to meet Governor Maxwell. Cuffe wrote in his journal that the governor "appeared to use us very friendly." However, the next day, when Cuffe went to the customhouse, there was a note from the governor demanding a report on the *Traveller's* entire cargo.

Cuffe was surprised at this attempt to interfere with his off-loading. Only the evening before he had shown the governor the license to trade with the Sierra Leone colony that had been given to him by the British government. The governor had told him to report to Charles Hopkins for his landing permit. Charles Hopkins had taken a whole day to find the permit. Then a customs officer was put on board the *Traveller* to oversee the unloading. His was "the first vessel," Cuffe noted, "that ever had been so waited upon in this port."

Cuffe spent the rest of November landing the cargo he had brought from England—general merchandise requested by the settlers. His small boats rowed back and forth from the *Traveller* landing firkins of butter, bushels of salt, barrels of mustard and pork, bales of East India and Manchester cotton goods, and boxes of hats, hard tack, candles, and umbrellas. There was also a keg of tallow for candles, hogsheads of tobacco, hampers of cheese and shoes, chests of hams, beef, and tea, crates of earthenware, and casks of liquor and hardware. There were parcels of paper, thread, seeds, and black pepper, plus baking pans, axes, iron bars, tin, silkworm eggs, and 258 iron pots for the missionaries.

All the books Cuffe brought from Britain he gave away free to the blacks. He gave his medicines to the dispensary. But he had to teach the settlers about the seeds and silkworm eggs before he distributed them. No one knew what to do with them. The governor was annoyed about the silkworms. He wanted everyone to raise cotton, not silk. Of course no black wanted to raise cotton—it was a slave crop. Cuffe hoped the silk would become the colony's cash crop—to be shipped abroad in return for necessary manufactured goods.

He sold his goods to all who "would buy and pay." But he preferred to trade with the blacks. The twenty white traders in Freetown monopolized all the commerce in Sierra Leone. They had no intention of sharing, or even dealing, with the blacks. One such white was the storekeeper Smith. When Cuffe sold him two hogsheads of tobacco, Smith insisted the tobacco was no good.

I told him I would take the tobacco back. He told me it was in the cellar, and it may lay there for a few days. I told him to give the tobacco up. He then seemed to incline to see if we had any better, or if any more arrived so as to be better or cheaper. And this appeared to me to have been too much the mode of his way of dealing. It showeth that he means to take advantage of me.

Cuffe's tin and hardware "sold very smartly. The people seemed to be eager to buy in a small way." Some paid money. Others bartered. Cuffe was especially interested in obtaining hardwoods and palm oil in exchange for his cargo. He hoped to create a demand for African hardwoods in Britain. Sherbro and rokel wood were good for shipbuilding, and camwood was used to make red dye. All three woods flourished in Sierra Leone.

The British were already trying to encourage the exportation of palm oil. Oil palms were plentiful in West Africa, and palm was becoming increasingly popular in Europe as an ingredient in the manufacture of soap, candles, and lubricants. The government believed that palm oil would be the easiest and quickest staple product to substitute for slaves as the basis for British trade with West Africa.

13

The Friendly Society

Paul Cuffe thought it strange that the British, who had outlawed the slave trade, would appoint a governor for Sierra Leone who regarded all blacks as slavelike. Governor Maxwell had even had a law passed that required blacks to be registered with the government—just like slaves. He and the rest of the white community in Freetown treated the blacks like children. They assumed the blacks could do nothing by themselves.

Cuffe knew better. But the black settlers needed more self-confidence. They needed to realize that they could stand absolutely alone without white help. It was they, after all, not the whites, who made Freetown a tranquil town, where provisions were moderately priced and plentiful so everyone could live adequately. Outside of Freetown the Liberated Africans were building roads and settling new agricultural areas. All this had been done without much white help. The whites just took all they could and left.

Even the missionaries considered Sierra Leone only as a way station. When Cuffe dined at the Anglican Mission, they discussed the "civilization of Africa. The British missionaries said what they would do if they were there permanently. I advised them to set the pattern themselves;

but they seemed to think their Church Missionary Society would not heave them out into the darkness of Africa for very long."

In December the black settlers were harassed by a new law. It required them not only to enroll but also to take the oath of allegiance to the Crown. The oath obligated them to obey the King's decrees in all cases. The blacks who refused were removed from the protection of colony law and threatened with the confiscation of their land and houses. Three times the settlers were forced to meet with the governor. Each time they refused to enroll and take the oath. If they enrolled, they would be subject to the commanding officer's order to march on any expedition whatever.

Five days after their last refusal, there was a midnight alarm. Unfriendly natives were coming to invade Freetown! The governor and chief justice were conveniently visiting Bance Island offshore, so the commanding officer took over the defense of Freetown. He sent out patrols and ordered the Royal Navy ship at anchor off Freetown to be ready for an immediate attack. But the natives refused to oblige. The settlers were not surprised. They knew that "unfriendly natives" only existed in the imagination of the whites.

After the failure of their fear tactics, the white officials decided that, if the settlers would not meet to enroll, they would not meet at all. The chief justice ruled that the settlers could not meet in their chapels during church hours while the Anglican Church was assembled. The Methodists held their Sunday service anyway and were fined £20.

The Methodists then decided to evade the rule by meeting in each other's homes as the Social Society of Sierra Leone. Harassment had finally made them aware of their need to be more self-reliant and organized. Cuffe saw this awareness as the first big step toward economic independence for the blacks of Sierra Leone. "I conceive this prohibition," he told them, "to be a maxim to make us look about ourselves and endeavor to help ourselves. And as we are made to seek, so may we find."

He then spoke to them about breaking the stranglehold of the small white minority by becoming economically self-sufficient and independent. The best way to accomplish this, he told them, was by establishing a black-run cooperative trading organization. They agreed. A constitution was drawn up and the Social Society of Sierra Leone became the Friendly Society of Sierra Leone.

As president of the Friendly Society they selected John Kizzell, who had already built an extensive business network in Freetown. Kizzell had been born in Sierra Leone, but was captured as a young man and sold into slavery in America. He escaped during the Revolution and went with the British to Nova Scotia after the war. In 1792 he returned home to Sierra Leone with the Nova Scotian settlers.

Cuffe approved their choice. He believed that, with proper leadership and a little help, the Friendly Society would prosper. He wrote to his English friend, William Allen, who enthusiastically replied with money and plans for a supportive group in London. The English organization was explained in its name: A Society for the Purpose of Encouraging the Black Settlers of Sierra Leone, and the Natives of Africa Generally, in the Cultivation of Their Soil, by the Sale of Their Produce. It would handle Sierra Leone's exports and funnel imports inexpensively into Freetown.

To see what produce could be exported and what natural resources developed, Cuffe traveled inland and made a survey of Sierra Leone's interior regions. He found the back country to be barren and rocky, but cattle and sheep were thriving on the ten-foot-high guinea grass— although some sheep were lost to leopards every year.

The thin, reddish soil looked poor, but the Nova Scotian farmers in the area said they could raise two good crops of Indian corn and buckwheat a year. And pineapples grew exceedingly well. Both the Indian corn and the pineapples had been brought to West Africa by the Portuguese from South and Central America, as had the manioc grown in Freetown along with other vegetables for subsistence.

Cuffe then rode a horse into the mountains to check on the plantations there. Most of them were now being tended by the newly Liberated Africans, whose huts dotted the area. He found "plenty of coffee bushes standing, but they are overrun with forest. They have corn fed plenty of fowl. They prefer them to wild game on account of the ease of feeding them. When they plant corn all they do is break a piece off the stalk and put it in the ground."

Traveling back to the coast, Cuffe stopped at Cocoa Bay "in order to survey if there was suitable places for making salt, but found no place without they were artificial made. The land itself appeared to be right leachy or sandy land." The West Bay area was much more promising with perfect locations for saw- and gristmills. Cuffe even offered to build the first mill for the colony.

There's a stream that has a fall power of over 20 feet perpendicular. I believe by carrying the stream in a trough 30 to 40 rods there may be a 30 ft. wheel for a gristmill erected which may go the year round. There's another fall of 25 feet perpendicular. At the distance of 44 or 50 rods it runs into a basin connected with the sea where logs, etc., can be conveniently brought to the mill. I am confident that there can be a wheel erected there for receiving the water over it 30 feet or more. Fifty feet of water would pass over in a minute during the driest part of the season, and in the rains there would be no lack of water.

Indeed Sierra Leone has the heaviest rainfall in West Africa—between 150 and 180 inches per year—although practically none falls from December to April. But there are often terrible tornadoes. All Cuffe's visits to Sierra Leone had been during the dry season. On his first visit in March 1811, a tornado blew down a couple of houses in Freetown. The next day "there was a fire cried, and it burnt 3 houses (they being covered with thatch grass in lieu of shingles), which appears very dangerous to take fire as it is very dry in Freetown."

But the worst part of the dry season, Cuffe discovered, was the harmattan, a hot, dry, parching wind from the Sahara Desert carrying clouds of fine dust called "smokes." The harmattan made men short-tempered and feverish. The close, hot, sultry air "seemed to take some hold of the upper part" of Cuffe's head. Many of his men took ill. Cuffe's nephew, Thomas Wainer, the ship's master, was "quite feeble with the fever. I myself," wrote Cuffe, "feel the symptoms, but am favored to keep about."

Cuffe called the doctor because "our family seems to be getting in a weakly way." Thomas Wainer refused to see the doctor. He was taking bark medicine and being cupped by an old woman who put "a plaster of flies nuts to the back part of his shoulders." At four in the morning he called his uncle and complained of a roaring, rushing noise in his head. He said that he didn't think they should stay in Sierra Leone any longer. He wanted to return to America to see his wife and children.

Cuffe put Thomas under the doctor's care and went to see two of his sick crewmen. But they were not in their berths. Cuffe, after some search, found Zachariah and Charles in a "rum drinking, noisy house in town." He told them "it was not worth his while to hire a nurse, doctor, etc., for men that were well enough to stand houses of mirth."

Then Thomas Wainer's knee became infected and

swollen. Cuffe sent a boat to the Bullom Shore to get leeches. Eleven of these bloodsuckers were brought back and applied to Thomas' knee with the help of a glass beaker. "If," said Cuffe, "they seem to be loath to take hold, wet the skin with a little milk. When they have filled themselves, they will let go. Then have a plate with a little fine salt. Put them in the plate and touch them to the salt. They will immediately throw out the blood and become limp. Then put them in clean fresh water, and they will be fit for use again."

After the leeches, a poultice of oatmeal, corn fodder, and beef relics was put on Thomas' knee. But Thomas didn't like it. He said it rotted his flesh. He preferred "green earth." Cuffe thought the knee should be cut "to let the infected matter out." But Thomas insisted on applying the green earth. And during the night he "became a good deal fuddled-headed." The doctor returned, washed the knee, put pepper leaves on it, and ordered a broth made out of chamomile flowers and bark for Thomas.

When Thomas' knee improved, Cuffe left him with a nurse who "fondled a good deal over him." Then, with the old year winding down, he set about fulfilling his neglected obligations. "We called our little family and friends together this evening, the healthy with the sick, and had a very agreeable time. The crew seemed to be on the mending hand and are getting upon their legs. But James Smith applied for some turpentine spirits for a bleeding at the stomach. I gave him some spirits of turpentine, and ordered him to take 5 drops night and morning."

The townsmen celebrated Christmas Eve by firing guns, singing, and dancing. By the day after Christmas, Cuffe noted that the people still "kept up a noisy stress with their drums, dance, and clapping their hands." Zachariah White, who had cured his fever with rum, wanted to celebrate the holidays by getting married. Cuffe told him that "if he could be steady and keep with the brig, he would never do better. But if he must marry, he must leave the ship."

Samuel Hicks also seems to be getting uneasy, and seems to be about to leave the vessel. I told him that if he goeth, he must run from the vessel. If he doth, I do not think that I shall kill myself in running after him, the sad tick. It appears that one of the settlers has a daughter in America and wishes to get her over to Africa. Whether Samuel proposed marriage or not, I cannot tell, but I conclude there's policy in it.

It was hard to keep a crew together on land. And the ship's master, Thomas Wainer, was not setting them a very good example. His nurse was taking such good care of him that he seemed to have forgotten his wife and children in New England. The Freetown settlers didn't care how many crew members Cuffe lost. They all wanted their sons to ship out with him.

Cuffe agreed to take one navigation student, "to become useful to the colony." But he could apprentice no others. There was too great a danger of losing them to impressment raiders. Once kidnapped they could never get away. Only a few weeks before in Freetown, two British sailors had escaped from their warship. A reward for their capture had been offered, and the men's own crewmen tracked them down inland in the bush and turned them in.

Cuffe told the parents to teach their sons a trade at home. Their best chance for advancement was in Sierra Leone. If only the settlers would "rouse themselves to more industry and sobriety, they would make better progress." Even in the Friendly Society meetings "more debating than business was done." Too many appeared "willing to laden other men's shoulders with burdens." Cuffe worried about the Friendly Society's continued commitment to self-help after he sailed. He decided to write them a message before his departure. The address advised them to

1. Be sober and steadfast at all times, "doing justly, loving mercy, and walking humbly."
2. Care for and teach the youth while "their minds are young and tender. That they may be kept out of idleness, and encouraged to be industrious, for this is good to cultivate the mind, and may you be good examples therein yourselves."
3. Be industrious and discharge obligations faithfully. "I want that we should be faithful in all things, that so we may become a people, giving satisfaction to those, who have borne the heat and burden of the day, in liberating us from a state of slavery."

Then Cuffe paid a final visit to the governor, "on the matter of improvement among the inhabitants of Sierra Leone, and on the propriety of obtaining grants of land, and of building a saw mill, and on his opinion on what encouragement would be given to those who would offer their aid and assistance to Sierra Leone." Governor Maxwell promised to buy Cuffe's American lumber and assured him that "every encouragement" would be given to all who sailed from America to become citizens of Sierra Leone.

Feeling he had done all he could, Cuffe ordered his uneasy and restless crew to prepare the *Traveller* for departure. They mended the sails, rove the rigging, and filled the water casks. The busy crew was soon added to by a chastened Samuel Hicks and a sober Zachariah White. They had become "sick of Sierra Leone" and wanted to go home to America.

Cuffe held public auctions to sell his remaining goods

quickly. He paid the doctor, rented out the house and lot he had bought near East Bay, and tried to settle his accounts. Smith's bill gave him some trouble. The white merchant refused to pay his debt to Cuffe in cash, insisting Cuffe take wood instead. Cuffe "thought it better to compromise than let the business run to a resentment. When men are like lions, we must be careful how we get our hands in their mouths."

Finally on February 8, 1812, Cuffe was able to pack up and board the *Traveller*. The ship was already filled with a cargo of African products, including a few last-minute additions brought by a native of Sherbro Island. He contributed "a plant that worms will not eat, some bark to make bitters of, and some root that was good to cover the bite of a snake and also to prevent the snake from biting you."

On February 9 "the Captain and Lieutenant of His Majesty's Navy came on board and inquired how I should make my course. Whether I should stand to the northward, or stand in the open. I cannot feel much liking for their conversation. What their meaning may be I cannot say." Cuffe discovered their meaning a few days later after the *Traveller* weighed anchor to sail home.

14

Homeward Bound

The *Traveller* sailed out of Freetown harbor with a "small wind" at 8 A.M. on February 11, 1812. Soon after a naval sloop also set sail. Four days later, on February 15, Captain Cuffe saw a "sail ahead, standing stern on. Breeze being small, I anchored." The sighted sail was the sloop of war, *Abrina*.

The captain of the *Abrina* sent a barge with his lieutenant to board the *Traveller*. The lieutenant "overhauled" Cuffe's papers and people, and left with the papers of the four Africans Cuffe had on board. He returned almost immediately with his captain, who commanded Cuffe to surrender the navigation student from Freetown and Aaron Richards—again. Cuffe's logbook, account books, and trunks were seized. And the *Traveller* was taken in tow back to Sierra Leone.

"I endeavored," said Cuffe, "to give the Captain all the satisfaction I could, but in vain." However, the next day the captain told Cuffe that "from reading the logbook and other documents, he concluded that Cuffe's motives were good and that he was not acting for personal gain but from principles. Therefore, he would discharge him and let him go." Cuffe thanked the captain and assured him that he had "the feeling motives of my mind."

The hawser was lopped. And we were left once more to steer our course, and he his. We both stood to the westward on a brisk wind. The *Abrina* out-winded us and outwent us, she being at or near sunset 3 or 4 miles to the windward. Then she bore down on us again. I was again boarded by the Lieutenant, who told me that he had come for me again. And that I must pack up all my things as before, and go on board the *Abrina*.

When I came on board the Captain told me he had overhauled his instructions. And he had no right to let me go, but should carry on to Sierra Leone. I told him I was sorry for that, but all to no purpose. We again stood for Sierra Leone. I opened the whole of the subject to the Captain, but all in vain. To Sierra Leone I must go, and to Sierra Leone he carried me.

On February 18, 1812, they anchored off Freetown. The captain went on shore and returned in an hour to tell Cuffe that he "had been to the Governor and had found all to be right and correct. Therefore, Cuffe was at liberty to go." He returned Cuffe's papers and personnel, made "a handsome apology, and offered his assistance." Cuffe accepted the use of the *Abrina's* boat to go ashore with his men. He wanted official papers from the governor that "will satisfy all inquiring people that all is right and honorable conducted, and will suffer us to pass un-molested."

Governor Maxwell received Cuffe cordially and signed the required releases for the four Africans Cuffe wished to take on the *Traveller*. With his papers and cus-toms discharge in hand, Cuffe ordered all the ship's empty water casks to be refilled and all hands to be on board by 10 P.M. in order to sail with the three-o'clock tide.

But after getting the water on board, Samuel Hicks

left the vessel without ever returning again. Although we waited until 3 in the morning with a watch on deck, we did not hear nor see anything of the said Samuel. We accordingly got underway, for had we not got underway at that time, we should have been obliged to have lain I know not how long.

I looked out of the Cape in the morn until 7 or 8 o'clock in the morrow before I bore away, not knowing but he might get in with the fishermen. But alas, no Samuel. Yet, I wish him well, and hope he may amend his habits to refrain from such of his ways as are not beneficial for him to retain.

> The man of sin,
> Who wicked hath been,
> Hath run his race,
> But got no grace.

Four days later, on February 23, 1812, a chase vessel came up to the *Traveller*. A boat was lowered and Cuffe's ship was boarded again for inspection. "After examining our ship and crew, we were discharged by the British man of war schooner to pass on our way." At last the *Traveller* was truly homeward bound after her twelve day's journey nowhere.

The sea was smooth, the weather clear, and the winds moderate. The *Traveller* ran under easy sail. Many fish were sighted, but none were caught. Schools of black porpoises escorted the ship, and there were plenty of flying fish. "Some flew on board where they met with a kind reception."

South of the Cape Verde Islands, they struck their first and only squall. It swirled down from the north and blew itself out in only an hour. Cuffe took in the "steering and reef" sails.

> If the wind comes before the rain,
> Clear the topsails and hoist them again,

> If the rain comes before the wind,
> Lower the topsails, and take them in.

A fine leading breeze conducted them across the Atlantic. Cuffe "improved it to the best advantage with all sail set." North of Bermuda they encountered a schooner from Baltimore "who informed us that the Importation Act was off, and that there were 2 French frigates and 1 brig on the coast." Cuffe shaped the *Traveller's* course for Block Island. He noted "many sails in sight. But got no more information. It appears that the embargo is in force and unimportation is on."

Jefferson's embargo against trade with France and Britain was called the "Dambargo" by shippers. It brought trade to a near standstill, and Congress was pressured to repeal it. When Madison became President, Congress passed Macon's Bill No. 2, reopening trade with Britain and France. Macon's Bill added, however, that if either country within three months stopped interfering with American shipping, the United States would stop trading with the other.

Napoleon seized this opportunity to outmaneuver Britain. He falsely led Madison to believe that he had revoked his decree ordering the capture and confiscation of all United States vessels. News traveled so slowly that Madison did not know France was still seizing American ships. So on February 11, 1811, he canceled all trade with Great Britain.

Cuffe was now unsure what his reception would be when he docked. He decided to keep the *Traveller* out of American waters until he could check with a customs collector in New Bedford. After sixty days at sea, Cuffe sighted Block Island off Rhode Island. He gave careful directions to keep south of Sakonnet Point and not allow the *Traveller* "to get within 4 leagues [about sixteen miles] of the land."

Cuffe then arranged passage on "a pilot boat belonging to Hamesset Hale, who agreed to take me to New Bedford and out again for $25.00." Cuffe and the pilot set sail at 1 P.M. on April 19, 1812. They sighted land at half past six. It was the Westport shore. It was already dark and quite foggy, so Cuffe decided to anchor at Westport and go home for the night. He wanted to see his family, and the pilot wanted to shelter his boat from a threatening thunder squall.

Cuffe rose at four the next morning to resume the voyage to New Bedford. They sailed south down the Westport River and turned east into the dawn. Fourteen miles away to starboard lay lobster-shaped Cuttyhunk Island with its single claw-like peninsula pointing across Buzzards Bay toward New Bedford. His relatives said the Algonquins had named Cuttyhunk "Land's End," but for him the island had been a beginning, not an end. It had pulled him away from land and launched him on the sea.

New Bedford had been his harbor, and now he hoped it would once again harbor his *Traveller*. He was not disappointed. The New Bedford authorities assured Cuffe that his brig could clear customs with an African cargo. Cuffe wished to return immediately with the good news, but the pilot refused to leave port with the wind blowing so hard to the northeast.

They waited until early morning, then "stood toward sea." By ten o'clock they had cleared Buzzards Bay and were entering Rhode Island Sound. Sailing west, they soon arrived off Sakonnet Point, where Cuffe had left the *Traveller*. She wasn't there! Continuing west, they sighted Cuffe's ship south of Brenton's Reef, heading toward Newport, Rhode Island.

When Cuffe finally caught up with the *Traveller*, he found his ship in the possession of the customs cutter. Customs agents had impounded both the ship and its cargo and were charging Cuffe with violating the recently reimposed embargo by bringing a British cargo to the United States. America was on the verge of war with England, and the ban on the importation of British goods was being strictly enforced. Cuffe had been trading with the "enemy."

Cuffe "called on the Captain of the cutter. He directed me to the Collector of Customs of the Port of New Bedford. I went to the Collector and informed him that all the vessel's papers were correct and that there was a correct manifest of all the articles on board. He then sent the Captain and the officers of the cutter and the pilot of the port on board. They found all the things to be correct as I had told them. I interceded closely for the release of the *Traveller,* but to no avail."

The *Traveller* docked in New Bedford on April 23, 1812, at 6 P.M. It had taken four days to sail from Rhode Island Sound up Buzzards Bay. The following morning Cuffe got permission to remove his personal belongings from his brig to take home to Westport. He felt "the need of the help of friends" and was advised to petition the Secretary of the Treasury.

Cuffe got a lawyer to write the petition and the customs collector to approve it. Then he decided to go to Washington, D.C., to present the petition in person. In hopes of influencing the Secretary to grant him an interview, he collected letters of recommendation from powerful community leaders in New Bedford and Providence, Rhode Island.

Cuffe sailed on the packet boat from New Bedford to Providence. In Providence he stayed with Moses Brown, the founder of the American cotton-spinning industry and Brown University. Then, armed with his documents, Paul Cuffe set off by mail coach for the seat of government.

I left Providence at 10 o'clock Sunday morning, April 27, and arrived at Washington 6 days or 100 hours later. I was 85 hours on my passage, or 3 days and 13 hours, and stopped 15 hours by the way.

When we stopped to dine along the way the servant came and told me my dinner was ready in the other room. I told him as I rode with the company, I would eat with them. So, we all sat down and ate at one table. This was the only objection that I met with. Indeed I was surprised to find in travelling through the country that the people seemed to have great knowledge of me.

Cuffe arrived in Washington, D.C., on the afternoon of May 1, 1812. He was very tired and went immediately to rest at the home of his friend, Samuel Hutchinson. Cuffe noticed that the capital, like the nation, was rawly new and unfinished. Designers had laid out magnificent plans for Washington, but in the spring of 1812, the broad boulevards were still only muddy paths. The Capitol was an uncompleted shell, and the White House was cold, drafty, and only half finished.

Ambassadors, Congressmen, and Supreme Court justices lived crowded together in uncomfortable clapboard boardinghouses, surrounded by swampy nothingness. And all this small cramped community talked about was war. The newly elected Congress of 1811 had many new "buckskin statesmen" from the West. Westerners had long complained that the British were paying Indians for American scalps.

Finally, General William Henry Harrison, the governor of Indiana Territory, decided to fight the Ohio tribes, led by the great Shawnee chief, Tecumseh. On November 7, 1811, while Tecumseh was absent, Harrison attacked the main Indian town at Tippecanoe Creek and won a shattering victory. The Westerners felt vindicated by the discovery of British arms on the battlefield.

The Westerners wanted war. They joined with the

Southerners to form a powerful prowar coalition in Congress. These "war hawks" got their leader, Henry Clay of Kentucky, elected Speaker of the House. And Congress resounded with cries for war. "I prefer," shouted Clay, "the troubled ocean of war with all its calamities to the tranquil and putrescent pool of ignominious peace!"

The war hawks were elated when President Madison recommended an immediate general embargo on April 1, 1812. They regarded it as a prelude to war and empowered the President to call up, for six months' service, 100,000 militia from the states and territories. Madison was won over. He agreed with the war hawks that war was the only way left to stop the British from harassing American ships and seamen.

15

A Capital Triumph

The day after Cuffe's arrival in Washington, D.C., the capital paused in its warmongering long enough to notice the exotic newcomer in its midst. Cuffe was greeted everywhere with great interest. Everyone was curious to learn what "the celebrated Captain Cuffe" had discovered in the savage, mysterious Dark Continent. But Captain Cuffe was interested only in presenting his petition to the Secretary of the Treasury, Albert Gallatin.

Jefferson had appointed Congressman Gallatin Secretary of the Treasury in 1801 for his able criticism in Congress of the Federalist finance policy. Gallatin had been reelected to Congress by the backwoodsmen of western Pennsylvania, after the Federalists took away his Senate seat. The Federalists claimed Gallatin hadn't been a U.S. citizen long enough. The Federalists didn't want him in the Senate. They were leery of the well-educated young Swiss who had chosen to pioneer the Pennsylvania backcountry and champion all minorities.

As Secretary of the Treasury, Gallatin carried out his program of financial reform and economy under two Presidents. He wrote *Synopsis of the Indian Tribes of North America,* and was an opponent of slavery. When

Gallatin learned of Cuffe's arrival in Washington, he agreed to see him immediately. Cuffe was welcomed with warmth and friendliness. Gallatin listened sympathetically to Cuffe's petition, then thoroughly questioned the captain about Africa and plans for relocating American blacks there.

When his interview with Gallatin was over, Cuffe was escorted to the White House to be cordially received by President James Madison. It was the first time a black man had ever been entertained there as a guest of a President. Madison had been looking for a solution to America's race problem, so he, too, was impressed with Cuffe's vision of an American settlement in Sierra Leone.

Both Madison and Gallatin found Cuffe to be unusually impressive. And Cuffe came to be regarded by the government as America's African authority. It was obvious that he had not knowingly violated national policy and broken the law. Convinced of his innocence and concerned with his predicament, they ordered Cuffe's property restored to him.

Two days later Secretary Gallatin invited Cuffe to his office and presented him with a signed public proclamation:

I, Albert Gallatin, Secretary of the Treasury, have considered the facts. It doth appear to my satisfaction that Paul Cuffe's voyage was not only innocent but was undertaken for most laudable and benevolent purposes, that there has not been any intention of fraud or willful negligence. Now therefore know ye that I do hereby decide to remit to Paul Cuffe all right claim and demand of the United States and of all others whomsoever to the forfeitures and penalties aforesaid without payment of the costs.

Costs were seldom waived by the government. The Secretary's offer to forgo payment showed how favorably disposed he was toward Cuffe. Gallatin also assured Cuffe that the government was ready to render help to promote the good cause he was pursuing, if it was consistent with the Constitution. And the government was ever ready to receive any information Cuffe could give or any ways he could point out to discourage the slave traffic.

Cuffe thanked the Secretary for his firmness and told him that unfortunately at present he had "no such information to communicate." Then Cuffe asked Gallatin "if I should continue my aid toward Africa, and I saw from the advice of friends it necessary to apply to the Government for assistance, would it be recommendable?" Gallatin answered that the government would render him every aid, agreeable to the Constitution, to forward his views.

Cuffe thanked Secretary Gallatin again for all he had done and wrote a moving letter of thanks to President Madison:

> I stopped short of my duty in not calling to acknowledge the favor that I received from the seat of Government, for which I desire to be excused. But upon serious reflection, feeling that there is an acknowledgement due unto the rulers of the people—certainly there is a greater acknowledgement due unto the Father of all our mercies. May the blessings of heaven attend thee. May the United States be preserved from the calamities of a war—and be favored to retain her neutrality in peace and happiness. These are the sincere desires of one who wishes well to thee, and all mankind.

The day after his successful interview with Secretary Gallatin, Paul Cuffe caught the 5 A.M. stagecoach to Baltimore.

> Being the first in the hack stage, I took the after-seat. In came a bustling powder-headed man with stern

131

countenance. "Come away from that seat," he demanded. I sat still. He took his seat beside me, but showed much evil contempt. At length a woman and girl made their appearance. I then arose and invited the woman to sit in the after-seat.

On our way, at the tavern stop, I was overtaken by Senator Hunter. He was very free and conversant with me, which this man, mentioned above, observed. Before we got to Baltimore, he openly accosted me. "Captain, take the after-seat!" I thanked him, and wished him to keep his seat. I note this for encouragement and memory.

When I arrived in Baltimore at 3 in the afternoon, they utterly refused to take me in the tavern, or to get me a dinner, unless I would go back among the servants. This I refused. Not as I thought myself better than the servants, but from the nature of the case, I thought it not advisable.

Instead some Quaker acquaintances "prevailed upon me to spend an extra day in Baltimore with them."

Cuffe met two teachers from Baltimore's school for Negroes.

They teach 107 children. This is a good prospect. I had much agreeable conversation with them on the mode of aid to Africa. I think some good may be done by this communication. In the evening I was to be called on by the stage, but was much disappointed in being left behind. So I arose at 2 A.M. At ½ past 3 went to the stage office, but the stage went at 2. Great disappointment, indeed.

Cuffe finally caught a stagecoach for Wilmington where he was "kindly received" by a few Quaker families. At eight the next morning he went on to Philadelphia.

Arriving at twelve thirty, Cuffe spent the next four days meeting with the city's outstanding black leaders and sympathetic Quakers to talk about Sierre Leone.

At 6 o'clock in the afternoon of May 11, 1812, I attended a meeting with the African Association in order to give them an account of Africa. It was proposed that there should be a Society gathered for the purpose of aiding, assisting, and communicating with the Sierre Leone Friendly Society, as well as with the African Institution in London. I believe that good will come out of this for Africa.

On May 13 at half past four in the morning, Cuffe set out for New York in an

accommodation stage where no fore notice was given. After a dull ride, I arrived in New York at ½ past 8 o'clock in the evening. I, being a stranger, could get no entertainment at the stage tavern. But a kind man took me to Jacob Barker's. Jacob friendly received me, and kindly entertained me, and told me there was a plate and a place for me. However, I thought it hard to throw myself on his hands, and took my chance among friends.

The next day Cuffe arranged to meet the black leaders of New York City in the African schoolhouse "where there is 100 children taught." They met "to consider which might be the best way to afford Africa some assistance." The twenty black leaders and their white supporters agreed "that there should be a New York society embodied, uniting with that of Philadelphia, Baltimore, etc. for the further promotion of Sierre Leone."

Returning from the meeting, Cuffe was introduced to two Methodist preachers, who asked if he understood

English. Cuffe replied that there was a part of the language that he didn't understand. He didn't understand those who professed to be Christians making merchandise of and holding in bondage their brother Christians. "This part I should be glad if they would clear up for me. We bid each other farewell without any further conversation."

Two days later Cuffe asked the same question before the Methodist Society in New York. "The members treated my question with rather a coolness." In the evening he repeated his question to the organizer and bishop of the Methodist Church in America and asked that it be given consideration.

Cuffe planned to sail home from New York on Captain Curry's ship. But the ship was detained for five days by a contrary easterly wind. Cuffe spent the added time visiting Quaker friends. He even traveled two miles out of the city to visit friends who lived in the "pleasantly situated" Greenwich Village. He met Dr. Ross there. The doctor had lived for seven years in Jamaica, and told of the Jamaican slaves "being gibbeted, bound on a plank, thrown down a steep place, whipped, hanged, burned and racked."

By noon on May 19, the wind finally changed, and Curry's ship was able to set sail.

We got underway at 3 o'clock. At 5 the vessel passed Hellsgate. At 7 we passed Throgs Neck, in sight of the Sands Point light, where we had to keep for the island to clear the stepping stones. Near the island we hauled more for the light to clear the Executioners rocks which lieth nearly 3 miles from Sands Point. Winds light, but fair. So ends these 24 hours with thanks to God, amen.

May 20 commences with cold raw easterly winds blowing strong off Crane Neck, about 4 leagues to the East off Lloyd Neck, Long Island. We continue to bear to the windward. Several sail in sight. We continued our course to the eastward, tack and tack, until 7 o'clock. We bore up for Sachem Head, but dark came on so fast we were obliged to come up for New Haven, Connecticut, where we arrived at 9 o'clock. Anchored, wind East by South, blowing fresh, and clouds looking heavy.

May 21 begins with light winds. At 9 A.M. thunder and showers of rain. At 11 A.M. moderate weather broadens, and wind hauls southerly. Reefed sails and got underway. Wind Southeast. At 6 P.M. the fog set in thick, then lightning, thunder, and heavy clouds with small gusts of fresh winds.

At ½ past 1 in the morning of May 22, the full light bore east, 3 leagues distant. Good wind, west by south, 3 sail in sight standing before the wind. Half past 8 arrived into Newport, Rhode Island. I called on the Customs Collector. He told me that he had orders to return my vessel and cargo without taxing me the costs. But on my departure I had to give embargo bond, and I had to pay wharfage.

Once home, Cuffe visited with thanks everyone who had signed the letters of recommendation which had been so helpful to him during his visit to Washington. Then he had to work hard to save himself from impending bankruptcy. His other two ships, which he had counted on to support his family while he was in Sierra Leone, had had bad luck. The *Alpha's* last voyage was a financial disaster. His uninsured bark, *Hera,* had rounded Cape Horn on a whaling voyage and never returned.

The *Traveller's* voyage to Sierra Leone and England had cost him a lot of money. But he felt it was money well spent, for it promised to be profitable for his people. He wanted to sail to Sierra Leone every year with a shipload of skilled immigrants and needed goods and supplies. He hoped to export African products to cover his expenses.

Meanwhile he would have to earn enough money to out-fit the *Traveller* again.

But less than a month after Cuffe's return to West-port, Congress declared war on Great Britain. Captain Cuffe could no longer count on transatlantic trade to re-coup his losses. Instead he would have to turn again to coastal trading and improving food production on the Cuffe farm. He prayed the war would be over by the time he had gained sufficient funds to return to Sierra Leone.

16

The Last Return

The War of 1812 was turning into the War of 1813 before Paul Cuffe was finally able to rescue his business affairs from the brink of bankruptcy. At last he was free to organize a second voyage to Sierra Leone. He spoke to groups of blacks in Baltimore, Philadelphia, and New York about the favorable possibilities of the colony. To spread information about Sierra Leone even more widely, he published a pamphlet on "present conditions in the colony."

Cuffe's Quaker supporters in England wrote that they could obtain a government grant of land in Sierra Leone to be settled by free skilled American blacks of known good character, brought and taught by Cuffe but governed by Britain. The more settlers he brought, the more land he would be granted. But the first group need only number about fifteen and be "persons of some property acquainted with the cultivation of Rice, Indigo, cotton or tobacco."

Cuffe answered with his usual counterproposal to establish a whaling industry, a sawmill, and the replacement of the slave trade with general commerce. Unfortunately, because of the war, Americans were forbidden to trade with the enemy British. But Cuffe was a

Quaker pacifist. He insisted that his plans for Sierra Leone could not be construed as assisting or giving comfort to the British war effort. He wrote to his English Quaker friend, William Allen: "Notwithstanding the declaration of war between these two countries, I hope that the chain of brotherly union in the true church is not shortened."

Unfortunately, Quakers had no control over government actions. So while the war dragged on, the only way Cuffe could return to Sierra Leone with his volunteer immigrants would be to persuade the British and Americans to relax their ban on trade with the enemy. A two-pronged offensive was needed—one in Washington, the other in London. "I believe if there could be a license obtained from the British government, it might also be obtained from this government."

Cuffe wrote again to William Allen, "If thee can intercede with the English government to grant a license for the brig *Traveller,* I shall endeavor" to get an American license and sail "the *Traveller* to Africa this fall. As here appears many familes much influenced to see Sierra Leone, I should wish for the way to be kept open."

On January 7, 1814, Paul Cuffe presented a petition "to the President, Senate, and Houses of Representatives of the United States of America." It solicited their aid "to grant permission that a vessel may be employed (if liberty can also be obtained from the British government) between this country and Sierra Leone, to transport such persons and families as may be inclined to go, as also, some articles of provision, together with implements of husbandry, and machinery for some mechanic arts and to bring back such of the native productions of that country as may be wanted."

The petition aroused such interest that the widely circulated and influential *Niles Weekly Register* and *The National Intelligencer* reprinted in its entirety the "singular and rather interesting petition at the request of several subscribers, who probably feel an interest in the success of Mr. Cuffe's expedition."

Bills honoring Cuffe's request were introduced in Congress on January 7, 1814. On January 25 the Senate voted 18 to 6 to pass the bill. The House did not. Supporters in the House stressed Cuffe's excellent character and the benefits for the United States of "the establishment of an institution which would invite the emigration of blacks, a part of our own population which we could well spare."

The bill's opponents were also eager to rid the United States of blacks. But they did not want the bill passed because "the enemy would never grant Cuffe a trading license unless it was considered advantageous to its interest." Therefore the bill would aid the British. So it was defeated 65 to 72. The British were willing to grant Cuffe a license, but could not guarantee his ship's safety.

There was nothing more Cuffe could do but wait for peace. It arrived a year later on February 17, 1815. Almost immediately he received letters from America's black leaders, congratulating him "on the happy event of peace," which would enable him to put his "benevolent plans into execution." The letters all included the names of families who wished to accompany Cuffe to Africa.

Cuffe at once put his other business aside and concentrated on organizing a second voyage to Sierra Leone. Finally on December 4, 1815, he was able to write to his English friend William Allen:

I have cleared from the custom house with the brig *Traveller* a small cargo with all the iron work for erecting a sawmill, a wagon and a plow plus thirty-eight passengers, 18 parents and 20 children. All which I hope may be well received in Sierra Leone by the governor—as well as the Friendly Society as they are provided with certificates as good characters. They are not too well provided with property as would be desireable; neither are they so much acquainted with the treatment of tropical produce as would be desireable. But believing them to be serviceable to the colony, I shall sail, through God's permission, the first wind after tomorrow.

God permitted the winds to blow Cuffe out to sea on December 10, 1815. They blew and blew. They blew so violently that twenty of the *Traveller's* fifty-four days at sea were filled with storms and squalls that grew in fury until they seemed certain to swamp the ship. Fortunately the sturdy storm-tossed *Traveller* managed to ride out "the most tremendous tempestuous weather" Cuffe ever remembered experiencing. The passengers wanted to die. Even the crew was seasick. But medicine and Cuffe's "close attention unto them" brought all to proper health.

Cuffe sailed into Freetown Harbor on February 3, 1816. He found, to his surprise, that no one was expecting him. Moreover, as an American, he wasn't even permitted to anchor. Cuffe went to the governor and was told that there was no trading license for him from the British government. He could anchor, but there was nothing to "secure him from seizure by a British man-of-war." His passengers, the governor said, were of course welcome to land, but his cargo was not.

Sierra Leone's new governor was Charles MacCarthy. Half Irish, half French, he had served as a monarchist in the French army until the Revolution forced him to flee to Ireland. There he joined the British Army and served in the West Indies until he was appointed the military commander of Senegal. When Governor Maxwell resigned in 1815, MacCarthy, as Britain's highest ranking officer in Africa, was appointed to succeed him.

Freetown was by then a pleasant, organized town with

stone and timber houses. Commerce seemed to be thriving. Even English goods could be purchased in Freetown at prices comparable to those in England. The town's social life was so dominated by the Nova Scotian Methodists that the Anglican church and school had had to close down, and the Church Missionary Society was concentrating its attention on the Susu mission.

When MacCarthy arrived in Sierra Leone, Britain no longer had much interest in its colony. The British abolitionists believed that the African coast was now nearly cleared of slave ships, and so there would be few Liberated Africans to set free in Freetown. The Liberated Africans were the only group in Sierra Leone that needed Britain's attention, and since their numbers were dwindling, government action could also decrease. This was the theory.

But MacCarthy soon discovered that the British abolitionists were wrong. When the Napoleonic Wars ended in 1815, the slave trade was resumed in West Africa. In the first year of peace, more than 2,500 new Liberated Africans entered the colony. The grass-roofed mud and wattle huts of their villages outside Freetown contained two thirds of the colony's population. They cried out for attention. "None of them raised a sufficient crop of rice or cassava for the support of its inhabitants."

MacCarthy organized the villages into a successful parish system of local government under the direction of the Church Missionary Society. He built a mission school and got a government treasury grant to provide clothing, food, housing, and tools for the Liberated Africans. By providing necessities, MacCarthy hoped to ease the settling-in process. The tools were to make them self-supporting contributing members of the colony. The Liberated Africans, however, took their free goods to town to trade. So MacCarthy's government-assistance program did more to stimulate trading in Freetown than it did to increase agriculture in the villages.

Yet the Nova Scotian settlers still distrusted Mac-Carthy. The governor had forced some of them to sell their land in order to increase the Kru settlement in Freetown. Since land was the only bank known in Freetown, the Nova Scotians deeply resented having to give it up. And they disliked MacCarthy's preferential treatment of the new immigrant groups at their expense.

When Captain Cuffe arrived in Freetown with nine new families, MacCarthy granted each American family a town lot and fifty acres of land to farm. Unfortunately the season was too far advanced for them to grow a crop. So Cuffe provided them with a year's provisions. He had already paid for the passage of thirty of his thirty-eight passengers. This additional expense meant a loss of more than $4,000, unless he could sell his cargo. But he was not even permitted to take his goods off his ship.

Obviously the English African Institution had made no advance provision for his arrival with this new governor of Sierra Leone. He wrote disappointedly to his supporters in England to say how sorry he was "to find no particular instructions at Sierra Leone" from them and without permission to sell the *Traveller's* cargo "the expenses of the voyage will fall very heavy on me."

When he received no reply, he forgot the cost to himself and concentrated on the successful settling of his new settlers. "Having the passengers so well received was great consolation to me." Indeed the prospects for their future looked bright. The Methodist school was thriving. One hundred and fifty boys were being well taught in the boy's section by Thomas Hunt, who had come from England with Cuffe on the *Traveller*.

The forceful new governor wanted a black schoolteacher also. He was trying to fill many offices in Sierra Leone with Negroes. There already were black sheriffs and constables, black clerks in most of the public offices and the printing office. They were entitled to every

privilege of freeborn citizens and sat in the courts as
jurors. The whites still had control of the colony. But the
blacks had equal rights, and as they became more qualified, Cuffe believed they would fill higher offices and
gain more self-government.

The Friendly Society was slowly moving the blacks
along toward the goal of self-sufficiency. The £70 sterling
that Cuffe's friend, William Allen, had advanced them in
1812 had grown by 1816 to £1,200. This increase in the net
worth of the Friendly Society was due to their commercial
pursuits, which Cuffe had foreseen would be the means
of improving both the society and Sierra Leone.

Preferential treatment for their products had increased trade with England. And good relations with the
natives had increased local trade. The Friendly Society
had decided to encourage this trade by building a trading
station upriver in the interior so the natives wouldn't have
to paddle their canoes all the way to Freetown. Cuffe
suggested that they increase trade still further by establishing trading stations with each of the interior tribes and
linking them all with roads. It might also, he said, "gradually wean them from being so strongly influenced with
the slave trade."

Cuffe wanted to wean Sierra Leone quickly from its
dependence on the whites. He had learned from his own
experience that even when you play the white man's game,
you cannot count on his cooperation. If Sierra Leone was
ever to become the haven he hoped for his people, then
the colony must become self-sufficient.

It had to develop its chief asset—Freetown Harbor,
the best on the west coast. But a commercial port needed
commerce. So Sierra Leone had to expand its foreign
trade with a circular trading route from Africa to England
to America. Cuffe believed that "if this circular route
could be kept open, it would help break the slave trade
which was carried on by the Americans under cloak of

other nations. And until this was put a stop to, it would be hard to obtain a general emancipation" of the slaves.

He wrote to William Allen about his promised but forgotten special government license so that he could begin to organize such a trading route. Then, in case the objection was to him and not the project, Cuffe suggested that a ship from Sierra Leone could be used. He had trained enough young men from the colony in the art of navigation. They could sail the ship. He ended his request with a plea: "I hope thee may not lose sight of the subject, for if it ever was in my mind and I see nothing that I think would have a tendency of doing so much good for the inhabitants of Sierra Leone as that plan."

Cuffe received no answer from William Allen either. There was nothing more he could do. So on April 4, 1816, he sailed home, arriving fifty-seven days later, on May 31, 1816. He found America worried over rumors of slave plots and uprisings. Southern slave owners were terrified that news of the slave revolts in Santo Domingo might incite their own slaves to rebel.

Cuffe knew that, if a few slaves did try to revolt, the Southerners in their hysteria would bathe the South in the blood of the blacks. He hoped that if Southerners could be reassured by a promise that their "dangerous" slaves would be removed to Africa, they might be willing to free them.

Up north the free blacks were afraid that if violence overcame the South, they would be engulfed too. They begged Cuffe to take them to Africa. Cuffe knew that the degrading discrimination of the North could be as crippling as the actual violence of the South. In Sierra Leone they would no longer suffer the daily indignities and abuse of despised aliens. They would be home, where equality was possible for everyone, where the future was bright with respectability and responsibility, and where life was not clouded by embittered despair.

But summer frosts had killed Cuffe's farm crops, and business was bad. Prices were high, and he had no money to pay for the voyages himself. Without a British trading license or some kind of government support, he would be unable to sail again to Sierra Leone. In despair he wrote once more to William Allen, begging that "the little seed that hath been planted at Sierra Leone should not perish." There was no reply.

The dream, which only a few months before had seemed so close to being realized, now shimmered away unreachably far from fulfillment. Cuffe had consecrated his life to making the dream real. He had given everything. Now he had nothing left, not even hope. The strain was too great. His body could bear no more.

As 1817 dawned, Paul Cuffe's always robust health broke. Confined to his house and finally to his bed by increasing pain and weakness, he called his family together on September 7 and asked them not to hold on to him, but to give him up and let him go. "Let me pass quietly away. I can no longer strive against nature." Then, at the age of fifty-eight, he "fell asleep in Jesus and is gone home to glory."

EPILOGUE –
The Lion Dismounted

After Paul Cuffe's death, Sierra Leone turned its back on America and looked inward. Those who had come to Freetown from the Americas became the social elite of settler society. The British, after Governor MacCarthy's death, gave up trying to control the colony. The Nova Scotian settlers ran Freetown, and the Liberated Africans were left to work out their own way of life in the outlying villages.

British naval ships were still freeing in Sierra Leone a steady stream of slaves from captured slave ships. The Liberated Africans were registered and apprenticed for three months in Freetown before being sent to begin a new life in a rural village run by a headman of their own tribe.

During MacCarthy's governorship, the Liberated Africans were under his direct control, and each village was supervised by a clergyman-superintendent from the Church Missionary Society This government by church and state could not last. Both missionaries and British government officials quickly succumbed to malaria or yellow fever in the "white man's grave" of Sierra Leone.

As the white administrators died off, the villagers replaced them with their own headmen, who ruled like tribal chiefs. In place of the supplies provided by the government during the MarCarthy era, the villagers banded together to supply themselves. Individual plots of land were farmed cooperatively. And while the men worked in the fields or in the village as craftsmen, the women congregated in the marketplace, where they traded prepared food and the main produce of the countryside— plantains, cassava, rice, groundnuts, beef, and pork.

In the evening the women came home to their white-washed mud-and-wattle huts to prepare dinner for their men home from working their fields of sugarcane, maize, cassava, or cocoa. After a dinner of fufu balls made from ground cassava and covered with palaver sauce, couples would either sit by the entrance of their compounds smoking and greeting friends, or they would listen and dance to the music of the drum and cowrie-decorated calabash.

By 1830 the Liberated African villages were economically independent and relatively prosperous. They were locally governed, adequately organized, quiet, and stable. By 1840 settlement on a tribal basis could no longer efficiently contain the more than two hundred different language groups settled in rural Sierra Leone.

Villages now had to hold more than one tribe. Tribal loyalty began to conflict with local loyalty, and the threat of civil war hung heavy over the land. Another Paul Cuffe was needed to reorganize the Liberated Africans. The need was answered by John Macaulay, the "king" of the Yoruba in Freetown.

The Yoruba was one of the largest and most closely knit tribes in Sierra Leone. If any Yoruba was "apprehended and brought before the magistrate for petty theft, and punished by a small fine, they paid the imposition amongst themselves, rather than see their countrymen committed to the house of correction."

"King" Macaulay established peace among the conflicting tribes by originating a supertribal organization in the villages known as the Seventeen Nations. A member from each tribe sat on the council of the Seventeen Nations. The council "supervised village affairs, settled disputes, administered justice, and maintained order."

The governor was afraid of Macaulay's power and complained to London: "It is a sufficiently disagreeable and embarrassing fact for the Government itself to know that those under its charge possess superior influence over a portion of the community, but it appears to me imprudent to let that fact become public."

But Britain finally had to admit that the Seventeen Nations was a superior system of local government for the Liberated Africans. The British colonial government, through illness and ineptitude, had failed. The Liberated Africans now governed themselves through the Seventeen Nations, as their Nova Scotian predecessors had governed themselves through Paul Cuffe's Friendly Society.

Having gained local political control through organization, the Liberated Africans went on to organize all-inclusive welfare societies to benefit everyone, dead or alive. Societies took care of the sick, buried the dead, and cleared land so every member could be economically independent on his own farm.

Commercial groups banded together in the marketplace in order to buy or trade in larger quantities than a single member could do alone. By a simple system of group saving, these commercial societies made it possible for the Liberated Africans to acquire enough capital to underbid the highly competitive Freetown merchants and gradually force them out of business. After taking over the Freetown trade, they developed an efficient system of distribution to expand trade with the interior.

Commercial skill moved the Liberated Africans out of the rural villages and into Freetown society. They acquired large amounts of capital, which they invested in

Freetown real estate to secure their social status. Between 1830 and 1860 the Freetown Liberated Africans were changed into a distinctive Creole society.

All the Creoles spoke *krio,* a "composite native language" that was basically pidgin English mixed with different tribal vocabularies resting on a West African grammatical structure that could naturally express native ideas. *Krio* was a language that reflected the history of the Creoles' cultural change.

Creole culture was also a composite. From the Church Missionary Society, the Liberated Africans had acquired a belief in the importance of education. A European education ensured a prominent social position for the Creole. And training in the law enabled the Creole to hold his own with a European, using the white man's own tools.

The Creoles adopted European education and dress, but they adapted the Christianity of the Europeans to fit native customs and beliefs. "They acknowledged the worship of the only true God as superior to any other, but could not resolve to give up their gods who they believed were created for the good of mankind, and therefore ought to be worshipped. The fact that God had given his son to mankind sufficed for Jesus Christ's inclusion with their deities."

The Creoles also retained the use of charms and the traditional tribal death celebrations. For, as one Creole explained: "This fashion we learned from our fathers. What they did we do too. This fashion no fit for white man, white man's fashion no fit for black man; you do the fashion you see your father do, we do the fashion we learn from our fathers."

Once the Creole position in Freetown was secure, they turned their attention toward developing trade with the hinterland. They set up posts at riverheads in many remote districts, and by 1880 the Creole commerce upcountry had increased the colony's trade fivefold.

In 1885 there was a worldwide drop in the price paid for Sierra Leone exports of rubber, palm kernels, and palm oil. The Creoles blamed the commercial slump on French territorial expansion in the north and tribal wars in the hinterland caused by chiefs who wanted to control the river heads.

The Creole Sierra Leone Association adopted a resolution calling upon the British colonial government "to maintain peace by force of arms, to guard the trade routes with troops, to define the frontier with France, and to send expeditions to open new areas for trade."

Britain already had an enormous empire. There was no interest in spending time or money in the "White Man's Grave" of Africa. Instead Britain encouraged British traders to establish private treaties with the chiefs of the interior. But the traders complained about "the system of partial annexation, which neither leaves the country alone nor takes it over entirely."

The British merely taxed the chiefs, and when they rebelled, their villages were burned down and shells were fired into their sacred groves. Critics called this British colonial policy "a coma interruped by fits."

In 1895 Joseph Chamberlain became Colonial Secretary. He thought the British should join the French and German imperialist "scramble for Africa," and not allow so much of the continent to fall to rival powers. Britain, he said, should have the "undeveloped estates" of Africa.

The governor of Sierra Leone in 1895 was a professional army man, who had fought the Pathans in India and the Zulus in South Africa. He agreed with the Colonial Secretary that the hinterland of Sierra Leone should be made a British protectorate. He thought tribal Africans were "ignorant, superstitious and uncivilized," but still they deserved to be protected from the "swindling" Creoles of Freetown.

Chamberlain decided that the new protectorate should

be opened up by a railroad and administered by a large force of police and supervisors. The money for this expensive operation would come from a native house tax. But the natives objected and started the Hut-Tax War. They "couldn't understand how Queen Victoria could lack money when her head was stamped on every coin."

The Mendes arranged, through the secret Poro societies, a simultaneous attack through the whole Sherbro, Mende, and Gallinas country. The attack was brave but hopeless. The Mendes charged in open country against British machine guns and were "grand sport" to shoot down. The Temne were better guerrilla fighters. But they also were slaughtered, and their chief was forced to declare: "De war done don."

The governor blamed the Hut-Tax War on the Creoles. The Creole press had attacked the tax, but they certainly had not provoked the revolt. The Creoles were afraid of the natives, who called them "white man's piccin." The Creoles defended themselves against the governor's slanders in their press.

The governor replied by destroying the Creoles' political power. He abolished the jury system for all noncapital cases, and he barred Creoles from the Legislative Council. Then he made them pay the hut tax, too.

The Creoles' economic power was destroyed when the railroad was built linking Freetown to Bo, in the palm-oil country. Palm products were much in demand for glycerine, margarine, and soap. The railroad opened up the interior to the British. It gave them the chance to squeeze out the Creoles, who up to then had controlled trade with the interior by their unequaled know-how.

> The train for Bo
> She no agree for go
> The engine she done tire
> For lack of plenty fire

> The train for Bo
> She no agree for go.

The train certainly seemed no go for the Creole. Large British companies, such as Lever, used their massive capital to get a monopoly of the interior trade. They could advance credit to the chiefs and buy in bulk to undersell all competitors. They then entered the retail as well as the wholesale trade to eliminate the Creole middleman.

By 1910 the Freetown Creoles' social position was destroyed when an exclusive new community "for whites only" was built eight hundred feet up on Wilberforce Hill, to escape the malaria-bearing mosquito. In Freetown property values and the fortunes of the Creoles fell together.

World War I drew Britain's attention away from Africa. After the war Sierra Leone, too small to compete with Nigeria and the Gold Coast, became an overlooked and neglected colony. When Britain shed its empire after World War II, Sierra Leone was among the first to go.

Independence put the Creoles permanently into the power of the protectorate chiefs. Outnumbered 100 to 1 by the protectorate people, the Creoles were finished as a political entity. Political parties now grouped around Mende and Temne factions. But all celebrated the white withdrawal by awarding Sierra Leone's first national medal to the malaria-bearing mosquito, for conspicuous gallantry in preventing permanent white settlement and making their country "the white man's grave."

Paul Cuffe would have been amused at such sophistication in his grown-up colony.

INDEX